TRAVELLERS

SYRIA

By
DIANA DARKE

Written by Diana Darke
Original photography by Diana Darke

Published by Thomas Cook Publishing
A division of Thomas Cook Tour Operations Limited.
Company registration no. 1450464 England
The Thomas Cook Business Park, Unit 9, Coningsby Road,
Peterborough PE3 8SB, United Kingdom
Email: books@thomascook.com, Tel: + 44 (0) 1733 416477
www.thomascookpublishing.com

Produced by Cambridge Publishing Management Limited
Burr Elm Court, Main Street, Caldecote CB23 7NU

ISBN: 978-1-84157-954-2

Project Editor: Linda Bass
Production/DTP: Steven Collins

Printed and bound in Italy by Printer Trento

Cover photography: Front: © vladphotos/Alamy; © Thiele Klaus/SIME-4Corners Images; © Getty Images/National Geographic.
Back: © Thiele Klaus/SIME-4Corners Images; © Sclarandis Piergiorgio/SIME-4Corners Images.

Contents

STREET NAMES

Where it has not been possible to find a street name, the author has described where to find each location or sight.

Introduction

Syria takes all its first-time visitors by surprise. Apart from the incredibly rich array of historic treasures, ancient cities, awe-inspiring castles and enticing medieval marketplaces, the country's natural landscapes are stunning and enormously varied. And far from being some dastardly 'Axis of Evil' as so often portrayed in Western media, the country welcomes foreigners and is an easy and safe place in which to travel. Rarely has a place been so unfairly vilified.

The first thing to stress is how safe it is as a holiday destination. Violent crime is virtually unknown and no woman need fear assault. Such things are heavily frowned upon as bringing dishonour to the family of the perpetrator, and it is no exaggeration to say you will be safer as a woman walking alone at night through the streets of Old Damascus than you would be in London.

The second point to emphasise is the huge variety of sights Syria has to offer. Within the space of a few days you can experience Roman grandeur at sites like Palmyra and Apamea, Byzantine churches by the hundred in the so-called Cities of the Dead, magnificent Crusader castles, the military and religious architecture of Saladin and his Ayyubid dynasty, exquisitely decorated lavish Ottoman palaces and even a rare Phoenician city. Landscapes range from wooded mountains that look almost Alpine, Mediterranean coastline and fertile river valleys to volcanic black mountains and the dramatic wilderness of the desert and steppe lands. Much of the countryside is surprisingly green – even the desert boasts seasonal pastures after rainfall – and in spring the hillsides and valleys are covered in myriad wild flowers.

Almost as unexpected as the landscapes and the sites are the Syrian people themselves. They are delighted to receive visitors and proud to show off their country. Yet they are not thrusting and clamouring like the Moroccans or the Greek Cypriots, and any hassling of visitors to buy souvenirs or to come into someone's carpet shop is thoroughly disapproved of by the Minister of Tourism. If he hears of such behaviour he immediately wants their shops closed down. Dignity is the watchword in Syria, and its people have retained theirs in spades. On the whole, therefore, your privacy will not be invaded, but if you appear to need help, they will gladly and tactfully offer it. The other aspect of Syria many

Westerners may find unexpected is the extent to which women are prominent in the workplace. Over half the graduates from Syrian universities are women, and they are senior in banks, government ministries, businesses and the professions. The dress of such women will be entirely Western and they themselves say they do not experience any gender discrimination.

The final aspect of Syria that is often overlooked by Western elements is its significant Christian minority. Christians account for at least ten per cent of the population and can be found in prominent positions throughout government, business and the professions. They, too, experience no discrimination as Syria is, like Turkey, an avowedly secular state, where religion is regarded as a private matter, and churches and monasteries continue to thrive without interference from the state. Syria deserves to be given credit for its unusual degree of liberality in such matters.

The lush landscape of the Ansariye Mountains

The land

Modern Syria encompasses a remarkable range of landscapes, consisting not merely of the desert expanses which the popular imagination might envisage from early paintings of Palmyra, but also of forested mountains, fertile river valleys, volcanic outcrops and a Mediterranean coastal plain. The country's economy is essentially agricultural, self-sufficient in cereals, fruit, vegetables and livestock.

In antiquity, the so-called Fertile Crescent fell within much of Syria, running in an arc from the hills of northern Jordan, up through western and northern Syria as far east as Iraq. This narrow band of territory had sufficient rainfall to be converted through irrigation into rich and productive land. In recent years, Syria's agriculture has expanded rapidly, providing cereals and cotton for export, and employing over half of the working population.

Carved out of four Ottoman provinces in the aftermath of World War I, the current state has two main geographical zones. In the east, bordering Iraq and Jordan, is a large area of steppe or open desert, crossed by the Euphrates River. The Tigris just touches part of the northeastern border.

In the west is an area of mountains and valleys where over 80 per cent of the population lives. The Anti-Lebanon Range contains Syria's highest mountain, Mount Hermon (2,814m/9,232ft), snow-covered for six months of the year. Along the eastern flanks of the mountain ridges are some shallow basins fed by streams. The city of Aleppo, once second town of the Ottoman Empire, lies in one such basin. Damascus, the capital, lies in another larger basin, irrigated by five streams. South of Damascus lies the Hauran or Jebel Druze, characterised by the black basalt of its volcanic lava outpourings from now extinct volcanoes.

In the extreme southwest lie the Golan Heights, Syrian sovereign territory lost to Israel in the 1967 Six Day War. An area of outstanding natural beauty, Syria calculates that, if restored, the Golan would increase the country's GDP by 10–15 per cent because of its fertility and its tourist potential. In the northwest, Syria also lost territory to Turkey. The Sanjak of Alexandretta was controversially transferred to Turkey by France, in an attempt to ensure Turkish neutrality on the eve of World War II. Syrian maps still show this as belonging to Syria.

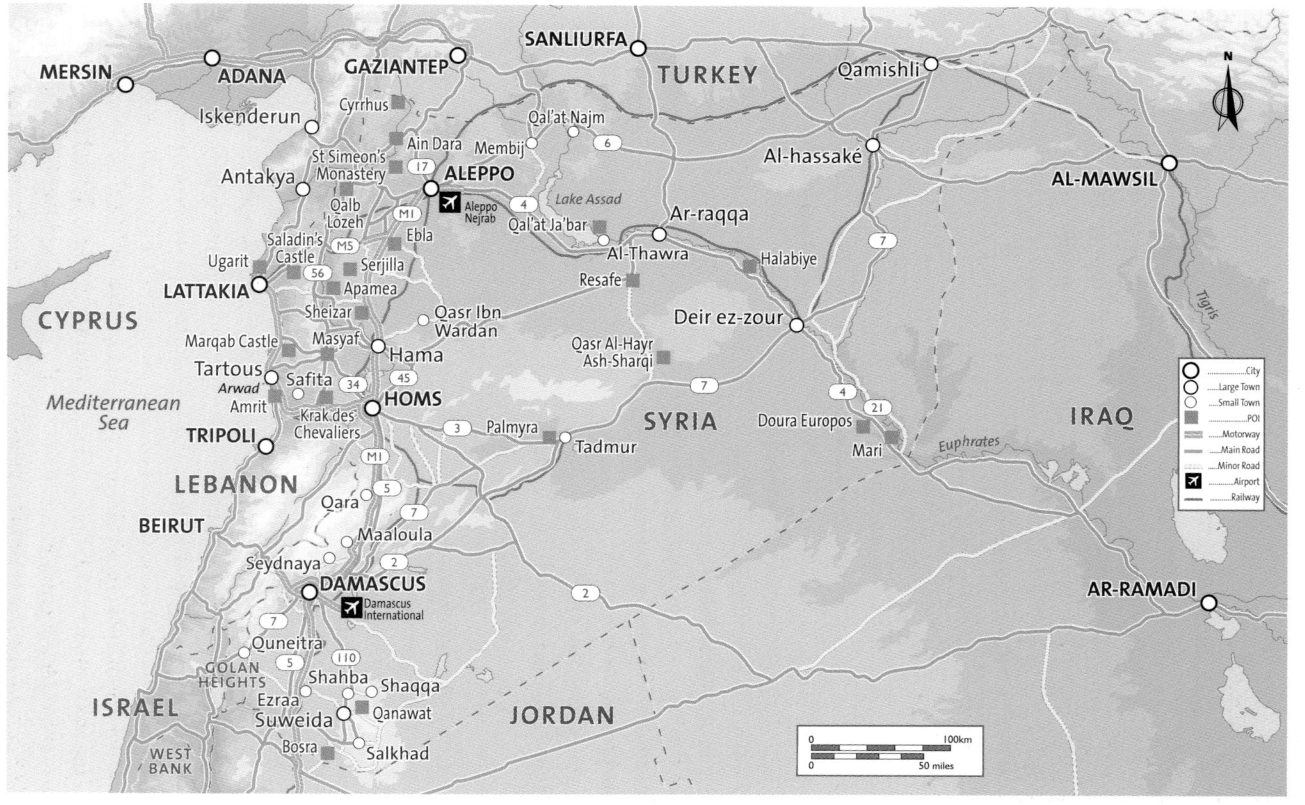
MERSIN
ADANA
GAZIANTEP
SANLIURFA
TURKEY
Qamishli
N
Iskenderun
Cyrrhus
Qal'at Najm
Ain Dara
Membij
6
Al-hassaké
AL-MAWSIL
St Simeon's Monastery
17
ALEPPO
Antakya
Aleppo Nejrab
4
Lake Assad
Qalb Lozeh
M1
Qal'at Ja'bar
Ar-raqqa
Saladin's Castle
M5
Ebla
Al-Thawra
Halabiye
7
Ugarit
56
Serjilla
Resafe
Tigris
LATTAKIA
Apamea
CYPRUS
Sheizar
Qasr Ibn Wardan
Deir ez-zour
Marqab Castle
Masyaf
Hama
Qasr Al-Hayr Ash-Sharqi
Tartous
Safita
34
45
7
Arwad
Amrit
HOMS
4
Mediterranean Sea
Krak des Chevaliers
3
Palmyra
SYRIA
21
Doura Europos
IRAQ
TRIPOLI
Tadmur
Mari
Euphrates
M1
LEBANON
5
Qara
7
BEIRUT
Maaloula
Seydnaya
2
DAMASCUS
2
AR-RAMADI
Damascus International
7
Quneitra
110
GOLAN HEIGHTS
5
Shahba
Shaqqa
ISRAEL
Ezraa
Qanawat
Suweida
JORDAN
Bosra
Salkhad
WEST BANK
City
Large Town
Small Town
POI
Motorway
Main Road
Minor Road
Airport
Railway
0
100km
0
50 miles

History

Pre-classical antiquity

6000–4500 BC The development of agriculture and the first domestication of animals.

4000–3300 BC The Uruk civilisation develops along the Euphrates. The first towns appear and the earliest form of writing is invented.

2900 BC The cities of Mari and Ebla are founded.

2300 BC Akkadian Empire of Iran reaches Mediterranean.

2000–1600 BC Semitic Amorite people conquer Mari and Ebla.

1760 BC Babylonian ruler Hammurabi destroys Mari, establishes the Hammurabi code of law, the earliest-known legal system.

1610–1580 BC Hittites from Anatolia destroy Aleppo and Ebla, then take Babylon.

1470–1450 BC Syria under the protection of the Egyptian pharaohs.

1350–1180 BC Hittite Empire extends from the Euphrates to the Mediterranean and from the Taurus to Damascus. The first alphabet is invented by the Phoenicians at Ugarit.

1250–1150 BC Independent neo-Hittite and Aramean kingdoms.

1200 BC Invasion of the Sea peoples, destruction of Ugarit.

856–612 BC Conquest of Syria by the Assyrians.

605–539 BC Neo-Babylonian Empire in Syria.

539–333 BC Persians under Cyrus capture Babylon and take over Syria.

333 BC Battle of Issos. Alexander the Great defeats the Persian Darius III and occupies Syria and Phoenicia.

Hellenistic, Roman and Byzantine Syria

301 BC Alexander's empire divided among his generals. Northern Syria falls to Seleucus. Antioch is founded as capital of the Macedonian dynasty. Southern Syria is given to the Ptolemies.

188 BC	Treaty of Apamea recognises Rome as the main power in the eastern Mediterranean.
64 BC	Pompey the Great annexes Syria, making Antioch the capital of the new Roman province. End of the Seleucid empire.
20 BC	The Euphrates is the frontier between the Parthians and the Romans.
AD **105**	Roman Emperor Trajan annexes the Nabatean kingdom and creates the Roman Province of Arabia with Bosra as its capital. Great economic prosperity through east-west trade in luxury goods; building of Roman roads.
193–211	Reign of Septimius Severus. Start of the Syrian dynasty.
267–72	Zenobia, Queen of Palmyra.
531–79	Persian Sassanids enter Syria and Chosroes I takes Apamea and Antioch.
611–22	Chosroes II repulses the Romans and Syria becomes a Persian satrapy.
622–9	Byzantine Emperor Heraclius launches a counter-offensive against the Sassanids and reoccupies Damascus.
634–8	Arab Muslims conquer Syria.

From the Umayyads to the Ottomans

660–750	Umayyad dynasty with Damascus as its capital.
750–968	The Abbasids massacre the Umayyads in 750 and Baghdad is the capital of their caliphate.
969	The Fatimids establish a rival caliphate in Cairo.
970–1072	Fatimids exercise control over Damascus and southern Syria.
1071	Battle of Manzikert; the Seljuks from Anatolia defeat the Byzantines and control all Syria. Fatimid presence only on coast.
1099	Jerusalem captured by the Crusaders. Frankish kingdoms created in Syria.
1149	Nur Ed-Din reunites Muslim Syria against the Frankish Crusaders.

1172–1260 Ayyubid dynasty in Syria founded by Saladin.

1187 Battle of Hittin; Saladin's victory over the Crusaders.

1260–1516 Mameluke dynasty in Syria.

1291 Fall of Acre. End of the Crusader presence in Syria.

1260–1400 Mongol invasions.

1516–1918 Ottoman period. Syria ruled by *walis*, local governors.

1832–7 Occupation of Syria by Ibrahim Pasha of Egypt.

1841 Europeans force retreat of Egyptian army from Syria.

1860 Druze and Muslims revolt against Lebanese and Syrian Christians. Massacres in Damascus. French landing.

The historic Citadel of Old Damascus dates from the early 13th century

1914 Ottoman sultan in Istanbul sides with Germany.

1916 Revolt of the Hejaz; Sherif Hussein and his sons call for Arab Revolt against Ottomans.

1918 Ottoman retreat from Syria.

1920 to today

1920 March: Syrian independence proclaimed; Faysal I becomes king. July: French Mandate begins; Faysal I exiled.

1925 Druze leader Al-Atrash leads revolt against French.

1938 France cedes the Sanjak of Alexandretta to Turkey.

1940 Ba'ath Party created.

1941 Official end of French Mandate.

1943 Shukri Al-Quwatli elected president.

1946 Full Syrian independence achieved.

1948 State of Israel created. First Arab-Israeli war.

1949–51	Military coups; military dictatorship till 1954.
1958	Declaration of the United Arab Republic of Egypt and Syria.
1961	Military coup. Syria now independent again.
1963	Ba'ath Party comes to power.
1967	Six Day War. Israel occupies Golan Heights.
1970	General Hafez Al-Assad comes to power.
1973	Yom Kippur Arab-Israeli War.
1976	Beginning of Syrian intervention in Lebanon.
1980–1	Syria supports Iran in the Iran-Iraq war.
1981	Israel annexes Golan Heights.
1990	Iraq invades Kuwait; Syria joins US-led coalition against Iraq.
1992–3	First official meetings between Syria and Israel at Madrid Middle East Peace Conference.
1999	Talks with Israel begin in the US over the Golan, then indefinitely postponed in 2000.
2000	Assad dies and is succeeded by his son Bashar.
2002	US officially includes Syria in 'axis of evil'.
2003	Economic liberalisation measures. Syria denies US's accusation of developing chemical weapons and helping Iraqi refugees.
2004	US imposes economic sanctions on Syria.
2005	Rafiq Hariri's assassination in Beirut; Syrians blamed. Syria forced to withdraw troops from Lebanon.
2006	Thousands flee to Syria from Lebanon to escape Israeli bombardment. Iraqi-Syrian diplomatic relations restored after break of 25 years.
2007–8	EU reopens dialogue with Syria. Senior US and UK politicians visit Damascus for first official talks in years. In late 2007, Syria is represented at US-led peace talks.

The Assad dynasty

Since 1971 Syria has been ruled by the Assads, a minority Alawite family from Qardaha, near Lattakia. From 1970 to 2000 Syria's president was Hafez Al-Assad, elected to power in a series of seven-year terms until his death in 2000 at the age of 70. His son Bashar has been president since then. Though much criticised and often unpopular, the Assad regime has undoubtedly brought a certain stability to the country, which suffered in the decades between independence in 1946 and 1970 from a succession of coups and counter-coups.

Hafez Al-Assad was born into a family too poor to send him to university so he joined the Ba'ath Party aged 16 and went to the Syrian Military Academy to gain a free higher education. He rose quickly through the ranks showing considerable talent and was sent to the Soviet Union for extra training, becoming head of the Air Force in 1964 aged 34 when the Ba'ath Party took power. He went on to become Minister of Defence in 1966, and, after various internal power struggles, launched a bloodless coup in 1970, after which he installed his own Ba'ath party loyalists in key positions in government.

Once in power he increased repression of all political opponents and used the state-controlled media to make himself into a personality cult, his omnipresent picture depicting him as a wise, just leader of Syria and sole champion among the Arab nations against Western imperialism and aggression. Neighbouring Iraq was ruled by Saddam Hussein's rival Ba'athist faction, whose methods of repression were far more brutal than Assad's, and the two countries had no diplomatic relations until after Saddam's regime was toppled in 2003.

Alawite supporters were appointed to almost all major government posts and increasing amounts of money were conspicuously spent on development projects in Alawite areas. Other groups felt more and more excluded from power, notably the Sunni majority who in any event saw the Alawites as an heretical breakaway sect from Islam. Growing economic hardship fuelled a rise in the Sunni Muslim Brotherhood, whose discontent spilled out in 1982 in the conservative town of Hama, with an insurrection against the regime. This was ruthlessly repressed by the president's brother Rifaat and at least 20,000 were killed. Since then the Muslim Brotherhood has operated in exile and the state security apparatus has increased its grip on any potential opposition through a vast network of police informers and agents.

When the shyer Bashar, originally trained as an ophthalmologist in London, came to power in 2000, this grip was initially relaxed, resulting in the so-called Damascus Spring where many political prisoners were released. The relaxation was short-lived, however, and Bashar's government still rules in an authoritarian manner, albeit with a lighter touch than his father's, whilst seeking to introduce gradual economic and political reforms. Bashar's wife Asma is a distinct asset in that she is a well-educated, Westernised and British-born Sunni Muslim who is becoming increasingly active in social and women's issues, in the same way as Queen Nour of Jordan.

Hafez Al-Assad is present still, even in this bookfair inside the Hejaz Railway Station

Politics

Syria defines itself as a 'Socialist popular democracy' with a 'pre-planned Socialist economy'. The Syrian constitution gives the president power to appoint and dismiss all government ministers. The president is also Commander-in-Chief of the Armed Forces and Secretary-General of the Ba'ath (Arabic for Renaissance) Socialist Party, a revolutionary party based on the ideals of Arab nationalism and socialism. In addition to the Council of Ministers, there is the elected 195-member People's Council, voted in by universal suffrage.

The original founders of the Ba'ath Party were expelled from Syria in 1966 when a new radical wing seized power, and subsequently established itself in Iraq, establishing a long-term rivalry between Damascus and Baghdad. The Syrian radical element then aligned itself closer to Moscow, a move which isolated Syria from many of its neighbours. Hafez Al-Assad ousted these radicals in 1970 and presided over a more moderate and pragmatic Ba'ath Party until his death in 2000.

Dr Bashar Al-Assad, the current ruler, known to be a shy and private person, had been studying ophthalmology in London when he was suddenly recalled to Syria in 1994 to be groomed for the presidency following the tragic death of his elder brother Basil in a car crash. Bashar was sent to the military academy at Homs and accelerated through the ranks to become a colonel in 1999. On his father's death a special law had to be passed to allow him to be elected president at 34, as the constitution had previously set the minimum age at 40.

Previously Head of the Syrian Computer Society and responsible for the introduction of the Internet to Syria, Bashar has indicated he is keen to implement banking and economic reforms. Some progress has been made; private banks have now been permitted to enter the market place, and the establishment of a Damascus stock exchange is said to be imminent. The pace of Bashar's reforms was initially found to be too fast by the old guard – the army, the Ba'ath Party members and the Alawite minority – and, alarmed by the prospect of their dwindling influence, they forced Bashar to slow down. He was the only candidate in a referendum in 2007, which endorsed him as president for another seven-year term.

Syrian media has been heavily state-controlled in the past, but there are now signs that censorship is easing, and a British PR company has even been employed to help train Syrian reporters in how to produce proper debate programmes. Subjects that were previously taboo are now occasionally aired, and even programmes criticising the regime are sometimes broadcast. Increasing numbers of people have satellite TV and can therefore tune in to other independent channels like Al-Jezirah.

Real political freedom remains illusory, however, and internationally Syria has become very isolated, accused by the US and the West of supporting insurgents in Iraq and supplying arms to Hamas. It remains staunchly opposed to the State of Israel, and peace talks about the Golan Heights, Syrian territory taken by Israel in the 1967 Six Day War, ran into the sand in 2000. However, in late 2007, Syria was represented at US-led peace talks.

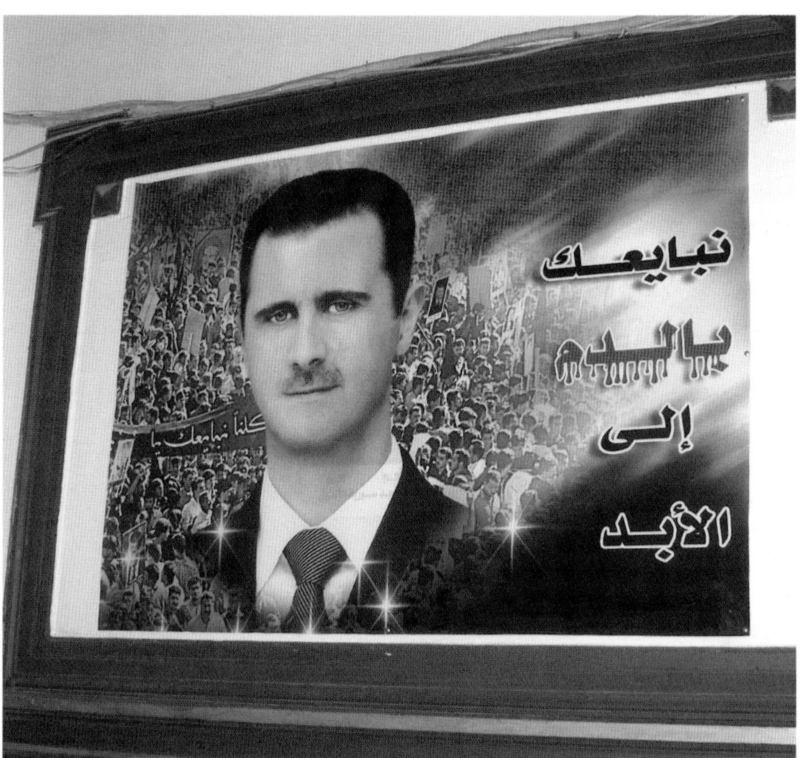

Bashar's supporters pledge allegiance to him in dripping blood

Culture

Both Damascus and Aleppo pride themselves on being at the heart of Arab culture, with their long and distinguished artistic heritage stemming from the rich and varied civilisations which either grew up here or settled here later as incoming forces. Always rivals, both cities have in recent years been awarded the accolade of Cultural Capital of the Arab World.

Architecture

Syria offers a rare opportunity to see all forms of architecture, starting with man's earliest attempts at building in ancient Mesopotamia, moving on to the Greek and Roman examples which abound, then the Byzantine churches and villages, next the Crusader military architecture, and finally the Islamic styles which developed right up to the end of the Ottoman Empire in the early 20th century.

Earliest examples

The art of building evolved here between the Tigris and the Euphrates rivers from the 4th millennium BC onwards, using the local material that existed in abundance: raw clay. Mixed with straw or gravel according to the local terrain, the mud was shaped into bricks. Local wood was very scarce and palm trees were not suited for roof beams, so cedar was imported by river from the mountains of Lebanon. The earliest-known dwellings were circular, with flat roofs, while temples and palaces were built on an acropolis, where sacrifices might have been held. These early cities were also fortified with walls and towers. Ebla and Mari are the two examples in Syria today of this early Mesopotamian architecture, their vast palace complexes conveying what opulent lifestyles the rulers must have enjoyed. At Ugarit, too, you can get an idea of the lavish wealth of the upper levels of society from the royal palace and the fine villas laid out round courtyards. The spectacular finds from these sites are displayed in the museums at Damascus and Aleppo.

Graeco-Roman ruins

Graeco-Roman remains are found in great abundance throughout Syria, from huge cities like Palmyra, Apamea and Bosra, to architectural fragments that pop up in the midst of cities like Damascus, where a Roman arch suddenly springs out on Straight Street or a row of Corinthian columns dramatically appears at the end of the Hamadiye Souk. Throughout the Graeco-Roman Empire the same principles of architecture and aesthetics were applied, with cities conforming to the grid pattern and the main east-west thoroughfare known as the *decumanus maximus*, off which the public buildings such as the baths, theatre and council chamber were grouped. The cities were enclosed within extensive walls with at least four main gateways, and monumental arches were often erected in honour of visiting emperors. The temples assimilated the local gods into the Graeco-Roman pantheon, so Zeus/Jupiter was identified with the Syrian Hadad. The site of Doura Europos is Syria's best example of Greek architecture where the temples show such blends.

Byzantine Christian remains

The Byzantine Christian period is marked by many early churches and basilicas, which would wherever possible be oriented east so that the rising sun would enter the apse and sanctuary. In Syria most Byzantine architecture is concentrated in the limestone hills to the west and north of Aleppo, where upwards of 700 Byzantine Dead Cities have been identified. They flourished in the 4th–6th centuries on the cultivation of olives and vines to make olive oil and wine, but were abandoned soon after when the trade waned, giving them

Artwork for sale in the craft souk

their name. Since they were built from the local stone, their condition is still remarkably good, giving them the rather haunting appearance of ghost cities. The most famous examples are St Simeon's Basilica and Serjilla.

Medieval and Crusader castles

Syria boasts the finest Crusader castles in the world, dating from the 12th and 13th centuries (*see pp112–17*), as well as many fine Arab medieval castles such as Harim, Sheizar, Rabadh and Masyaf.

Islamic period

The various Muslim rulers endowed Syria with many beautiful religious buildings, not only mosques, but also madrasas (religious colleges), mausoleums and *bimaristans* (religious teaching hospitals). There are also numerous fine examples of secular architecture, such as palaces, hammams (baths), souks (markets) and *khans* (caravanserais). The best examples are concentrated in Damascus and Aleppo. The Great Umayyad Mosque, built in the 8th century, and the Tekkiye Suleymaniye built by Sinan 800 years later, represent the high points. Both are in Damascus.

Art

Syria enjoys an active modern art scene, and, whilst not as thriving as in Egypt, it has benefited from the addition to its native artists of a considerable artistic refugee community from both Iraq and Lebanon, who have found in Syria a haven from the turbulence of their own countries. Calligraphy, sculpture and decorative arts like ceramic tiles have long and distinguished histories in the region, but the Western custom of painting onto canvas only began here after Napoleon's invasion of Egypt in 1798, which led in turn to an invasion of European artists keen to capture the 'Orientalist' spirit on canvas, and whose artistic methods were then imitated locally.

The easiest places to view modern art are in the Damascus and Aleppo National Museums, where large upstairs areas are devoted to displays of modern painting and sculpture. Damascus also has a number of smaller private galleries, and paintings by modern local artists are on sale in shops along Straight Street in the Old City and in the Suleymaniye Tekke shopping galleries behind the National Museum.

Theatre and cinema

Syria can boast its own film industry, despite the rigours of state censorship which imposes considerable restrictions on any films thought to raise controversial political, social or sexual issues. Some of the more critical films have had to be made abroad, in Europe especially, while the general diet of regular film material on view within the country tends to be a lot of imported kung fu-type movies, high on action and low on content. Cinema audiences tend to be young and male. The foreign cultural institutes also show foreign films, notably the French Cultural Institute and the Goethe Institut, and their programmes are advertised in the local press.

Local theatrical performances are limited and tend to be staged as part of festivals such as the Silk Road Festival and the Palmyra Festival, consisting of colourful and melodramatic re-enactments of historical episodes from the glorious past, entertaining to watch but of little artistic merit.

Darwish Pasha Mosque (1572) in early Ottoman style

Festivals and events

There are not many special festivals in Syria above and beyond the usual religious festivals that occur in all Muslim countries. The few that are worth singling out are:

Amrit Festival for Culture and Arts is held annually by the Ministry of Culture 28–31 August, to raise awareness of Amrit's importance as an early Phoenician site. Music, dancing and singing in the stadium.

Bosra Festival is held every two years (odd years) in the Roman theatre in early September. It lasts for around 15 days and includes dancing, drama, music and singing.

Palmyra Festival has been held twice a year since 1993, usually 2–5 May and then again at the end of September during the Silk Road Festival, organised by the Ministry of Tourism. It includes folkloric dancing and singing performances, together with horse and camel races in the racecourse below the Arab fort.

Religious holidays

On top of the fixed secular holidays (*see p153*) are the Muslim feast days, which move according to the lunar calendar, thereby going backwards by 10 or 11 days every year in the Western Gregorian calendar.

In 2007–8, Eid Al-Fitr will take place from 1–3 October 2008, while in 2008–9, the holidays are estimated to be on the following days:

Eid Al-Adha	7–10 December
Al-Hijra	28 December
Mawlid An-Nabi	8 March
Eid Al-Fitr	20–22 September

The various Christian sects celebrate Easter and their particular saints' days, when they will close their shops and businesses, while the Muslim shops and businesses will remain open.

Ramadan

Ramadan is the ninth month of the Islamic lunar calendar and is 30 days of fasting from daybreak to sundown. As well as abstaining from food, the devout Muslim must also abstain from drinking, smoking and sexual intercourse, i.e. all bodily pleasures, during daylight hours. Of course, after sundown all these bodily pleasures are enjoyed all the more, and there is more conspicuous consumption of meat and food generally during Ramadan than at any other time. Visiting Syria during Ramadan is not a problem, as most restaurants continue to serve food and drink. You will, however, notice that opening hours are foreshortened and that tempers are also shorter. And even as a non-Muslim, it is a courtesy not to eat and drink or smoke publicly during Ramadan, out of respect for the holy month.

Far from being viewed with horror by Muslims, Ramadan is generally looked forward to as the high point of the year, when there are more parties and socialising than at any other time. Eid Al-Fitr is the feast holiday period that follows the end of Ramadan (literally 'the breaking of the fast'), and the other feast of Eid Al-Adha (Feast of the Sacrifice) marks Abraham's willingness to sacrifice his son Isaac to God.

A poster for the Krak des Chevaliers theatre

Syrian poets and philosophers

Syria boasts a great wealth of literary genius, of which the following is just a flavour.

Al-Mutanabbi (915–65)

The most popular and widely quoted poet of the Arab world, Al-Mutanabbi was made poet laureate at the court of his patron, Sayf Ad-Dawla, ruler of the breakaway Hamdanid dynasty of Aleppo. His poetry is frequently described by Arab critics as 'the height of perfection', and his total mastery of the Arabic language is difficult to convey in translation, as Arabic's tendency to hyperbole is so alien to English natural understatement. His style is full of rhetoric and rich with metaphor, yet he was the son of a simple water carrier.

'My songs gave eyes to the blind, ears to the deaf,
Set the critics flapping like nightbirds,
Set me at rest all night on my bed.
And pay me well if I write you a eulogy.
The flatterers will come to you mouthing it.
And desert every voice but mine, for I
Am the singing lark, the rest are echo.'

(Translated by H Howarth and I Shukrallah.)

Al-Ma'arri (973–1057)

In complete contrast to Al-Mutanabbi, the poet-philosopher Al-Ma'arri shunned society, living and dying in his native town of Ma'arat An-Nu'man. Orphaned and made blind aged four by an attack of smallpox, his poems are sad and cynical, showing a great sensitivity to man's suffering. His *Treatise on Forgiveness* is believed to have directly influenced Dante's *Divine Comedy*. He wrote of doubts and contradictions in *Luzum ma yalzam* (*The Necessity of what is not Necessary*):

'And never doth man attain to swim on a full-born tide
Of glory but after he was sunken in miseries.
It hindereth not my mind from sure expectations of
A mortal event, that I am mortal and mortal's son.
I swerve and they miss their mark, the arrows Life aims at me,
But sped they from bows of Death, not thus they would see me serve.

The strange camels jealously are
driven from the pond
of Death.'
(Translated by R A Nicholson.)

Ibn 'Arabi (1165–1240)

The great Sufi mystic philosopher Muhiyaddin Muhammad Ibn 'Arabi, having travelled from his birthplace in Spain across North Africa and Arabia, settled for the last 20 years of his life in Damascus and is buried in the suburb of Salihiye in a tomb below the Selimi Mosque, much visited by Sufi pilgrims paying devotions to their Shaikh. His teachings spread east as far as China and north into Anatolia. Extraordinarily complex, he wrote highly symbolic treatises attempting to express man's relationship with himself and God.

'I am no one in existence but myself, so –
Whom do I treat as foe and whom do I treat as friend? [...]
Why defend my station? It matters little to me; what do I care?
For I am in love with none other than myself, and my very separation is my union.
Do not blame me for my passion. I am inconsolable over the one who has fled me.'
(Translated by Angela Jaffray.)

Nizar Qabbani (1923–98)

Syria's greatest love poet, who grew up in a Damascus courtyard house, bemoaned in later life the tragedy of the Arab world:

'How do people distinguish between gardens and dunghills?
Each day we regress a thousand years.'
And:
'No regime could arrest my poems for they are dipped in the oil of freedom.'
(Translated by Lena Jayyusi and Sharif Elmusa.)

The tomb of Ibn 'Arabi in Damascus

Highlights

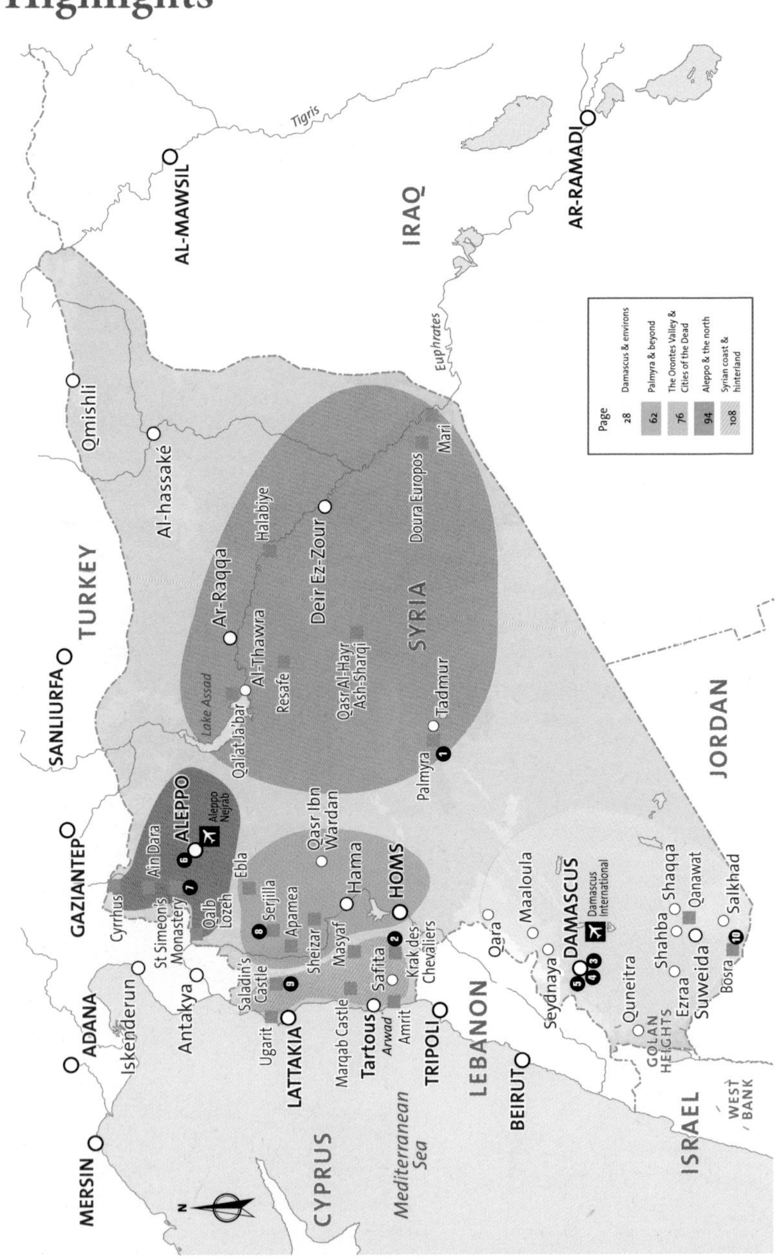

MERSIN
ADANA
Iskenderun
Antakya
GAZIANTEP
SANLIURFA
TURKEY
AL-MAWSIL
Tigris
IRAQ
AR-RAMADI
Euphrates
Qmishli
Al-hassaké
CYPRUS
Mediterranean Sea
LATTAKIA
Ugarit
Saladin's Castle
Cyrrhus
St Simeon's Monastery
Ain Dara
Qalb Lozeh
ALEPPO
Aleppo Nejrab
Ebla
Serjilla
Apamea
Sheizar
Masyaf
Hama
Qasr Ibn Wardan
HOMS
Krak des Chevaliers
Safita
Marqab Castle
Tartous
Arwad
Amrit
TRIPOLI
LEBANON
BEIRUT
Lake Assad
Qal'at Ja'bar
Al-Thawra
Ar-Raqqa
Resafe
Halabiye
Deir Ez-Zour
Qasr Al-Hayr Ash-Sharqi
SYRIA
Tadmur
Palmyra
Doura Europos
Mari
Qara
Maaloula
Seydnaya
DAMASCUS
Damascus International
Quneitra
GOLAN HEIGHTS
Ezraa
Shahba
Shaqqa
Suweida
Qanawat
Bosra
Salkhad
JORDAN
ISRAEL
WEST BANK
N
Page
28 Damascus & environs
62 Palmyra & beyond
76 The Orontes Valley & Cities of the Dead
94 Aleppo & the north
108 Syrian coast & hinterland

1. Walking at dawn among the temples of the Roman caravan city of Palmyra.
2. Strolling round the ramparts of the world's best-preserved Crusader castle, Krak des Chevaliers.
3. Absorbing the tranquillity of Damascus's Great Umayyad Mosque from its shaded courtyard and gazing at its mosaics depicting paradise.
4. Discovering the exquisitely restored Ottoman palaces of the walled Old City of Damascus.
5. Marvelling at the colourful synagogue from Doura Europos reconstructed in situ at the Damascus National Museum.
6. Exploring the narrow winding alleys of Aleppo's medieval souk.
7. Climbing up the Pilgrims' Way to reach the spectacular basilica complex of St Simeon, the hermit who lived for over 30 years on top of his pillar.
8. Wandering at sunset round the hauntingly deserted village of Serjilla, one of the many hundreds of ruined Byzantine Cities of the Dead.
9. Visiting the 12th-century Saladin's Castle on its dramatic outcrop in the heavily wooded Ansariye Mountains.
10. Happening upon the magnificent Roman theatre at Bosra, concealed inside a 13th-century Ayyubid citadel.

The ruins of Palmyra at sunset

Suggested itineraries

The following is a range of itineraries, from a long weekend to an extensive 16-night tour. Although the bus network in Syria is efficient and well organised, it is preferable to hire your own car in order to benefit most from these itineraries.

Long weekend (four nights)

Day 1 Arrive in Damascus and explore the Old City and National Museum.

Day 2 Drive to Palmyra (three hours) after lunch.

Day 3 Explore the ruins in the morning, then after lunch drive to Krak des Chevaliers (two hours).

Day 4 Spend the morning at the Crusader castle, and return to Damascus (two hours) after lunch.

One week

With a total distance of 1,200km (745 miles), this is a fairly intensive itinerary.

Days 1–2 Arrive in Damascus and explore the Old City.

Day 3 Drive from Damascus to Lattakia via Maaloula, Krak des Chevaliers and Marqab Castle.

Day 4 Drive from Lattakia to Aleppo via Ugarit, Saladin's Castle and St Simeon's basilica.

Day 5 See Aleppo, citadel and Old City.

Day 6 Drive from Aleppo to Palmyra, via Ebla and Hama.

Day 7 Complete visit of Palmyra, drive to Damascus.

12 days

At 2,200km (1,370 miles), another intensive tour.

Days 1–2 Arrive in Damascus and explore the Old City.

Day 3 Excursion south to the Hauran region and Bosra; return to Damascus.

Day 4 Drive from Damascus to Safita via Seydnaya and Maaloula, and Krak des Chevaliers.

Day 5 Drive from Safita to Lattakia, via Amrit, Tartous and Marqab Castle.

Day 6 Drive from Lattakia to Hama via Ugarit, Saladin's Castle and Apamea.

Day 7 Drive from Hama to Aleppo, via Ma'arrat An-Nu'man, Serjilla, Al-Bara, Qalb Lozeh and St Simeon's basilica.

Day 8 See Aleppo, citadel and Old City.

Day 9 Drive from Aleppo to Deir Ez-Zour, via Resafe, Ar-Raqqa and Halabiye.

Day 10 Drive from Deir Ez-Zour to Palmyra, also visiting Mari and Doura Europos.

Day 11 Enjoy a complete day at Palmyra.

Day 12 Return to Damascus.

16 days

This option offers a more leisurely pace, covering 2,000km (1,240 miles).

Days 1–3 Arrive in Damascus and explore the Old City.

Day 4 Drive from Damascus to Bosra, via Shahba, Shaqqa, Qanawat and Suweida.

Day 5 Drive from Bosra to Palmyra, via Ezraa and Maaloula.

Day 6 Enjoy a full day at Palmyra.

Day 7 Drive from Palmyra to Safita, via Homs and Krak des Chevaliers.

Day 8 Drive from Safita to Lattakia via Safita Castle, Amrit, Tartous and Marqab Castle.

Day 9 Based at Lattakia, visit Ugarit and Saladin's Castle.

Day 10 Drive from Lattakia to Aleppo via Qalb Lozeh church, Baqirha and Breij Monastery.

Days 11–12 Sightsee in Aleppo.

Day 13 Make an excursion to Cyrrhus, Ain Dara and St Simeon.

Day 14 Drive from Aleppo to Hama, via Ebla, Al-Bara, Serjilla and Ma'arrat An-Nu'man.

Day 15 Visit Hama, Apamea and Masyaf Castle, and overnight in Hama again.

Day 16 Return to Damascus via Mar Mousa monastery.

The Crusader fortress, Krak des Chevaliers, is one of the most important medieval military buildings in the world

Damascus and environs

Voted the Cultural Capital of the Arab world for 2008, much attention is now focused on the age-old charms of Damascus, and funds will be channelled into further beautifying the city. For centuries, Damascus has been somewhere people have come for pleasure (for commerce they head to Aleppo): the pleasure of eating, for example, and the pleasure of ornamentation as illustrated in the palaces and in craftsmanship of the most magnificent materials, such as damask cloth. Also a city rich in biblical associations, about a dozen religious communities coexist peacefully here.

Damascus lies at a surprising altitude of 690m (2,264ft), giving it cooling breezes in the summer, and, as you head south, the terrain remains mountainous, culminating in the volcanic outcrop of the Jebel Druze, where the best '*araq* is produced. The landscapes have an austere charm with vast bare plains and random outcrops of volcanic basalt, yet have great fertility and in Roman times were a breadbasket for the armies of the Empire, producing fields of wheat. The volcanic slopes of the Jebel Druze are famous for their apple trees and their vines, a legacy of the French Mandate.

In the 2nd century the region flourished and the population boomed, building towns in the imperial style, embellished with grand public institutions and rich private villas, whose fine mosaic floors remain today on display in the region's museums. Bosra, as capital of the province, was the grandest, but other towns such as Suweida, Shahba and Qanawat were also major centres.

Later, Christianity obtained a firm foothold, and many towns boasted a

The steep ascent to Mar Mousa monastery in the Qalamoun Mountains

church or even several churches. The unusual church of St George at Ezraa, erected on the site of a pagan temple early in the 6th century, is one of the oldest still in use in Syria (*see p52*). The biggest concentration of Christian communities in Syria is, however, to be found about an hour's drive north of Damascus in the Qalamoun Mountains, where monastic communities still survive as they have, little changed, for centuries (*see pp56–9*).

Several days will be needed in the region for an adequate introduction; one touring south of Damascus, one touring to the north, with two or three days spent exploring Damascus itself. Damascus can be used as a base, with a one-day trip to the south and one to the north. Or if you prefer, Bosra offers good accommodation as a base for the southern Roman and Druze tour, as does Maaloula for the northern Christian tour.

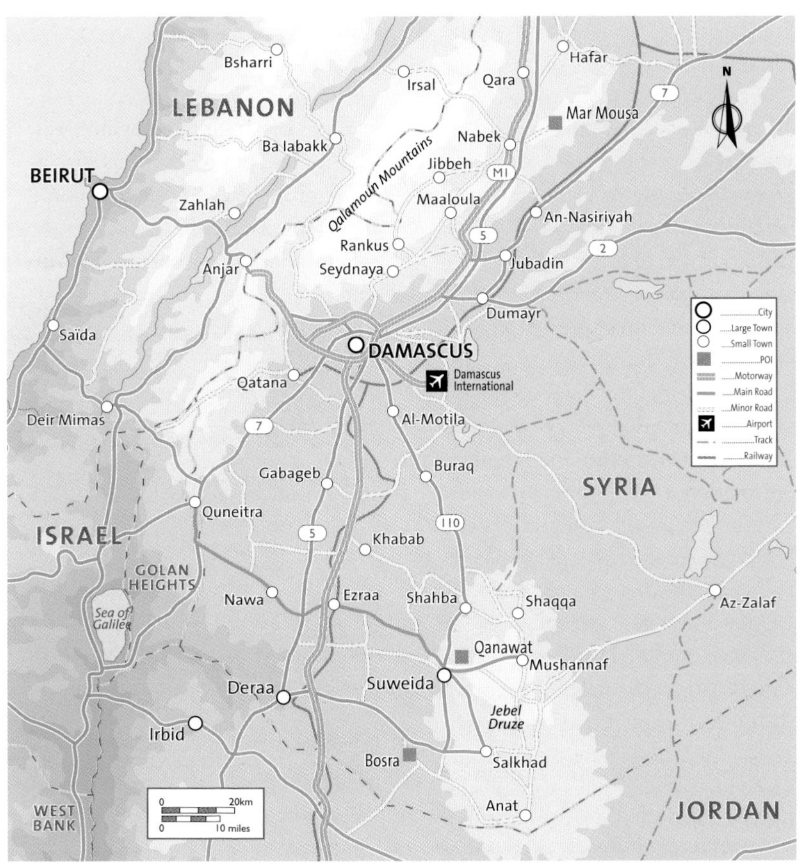

Damascus city

A minimum of two full days is needed to see the main sights of the city, of which one and a half days should be devoted to the Old City. Within the Old City, one full day should be spent in the Muslim Quarter, with its Great Umayyad Mosque, souks, madrasas, palaces and museums, one half day in the Christian Quarter exploring the churches, chapels and Straight Street, and a half day should be devoted to the National Museum plus the nearby Handicraft Souk and the Suleymaniye Tekke centre.

On one evening, to get your bearings and fully appreciate the setting, you should take a taxi up to Jebel Qassioun, the bare outcrop that rises above the city to the north. At night the Old City is easy to pick out from the concentration of green lights of the mosques, with the vast and unmistakeable shape of the Umayyad Mosque at its heart.

The arrival of the Romans totally altered the physiognomy of Damascus. The new rulers of the Orient built a city enclosed by a wall pierced by seven gates and designed on a grid pattern with roads criss-crossing the main east-west axis (the *decumanus*), later to become the Street Called Straight. On the ancient pagan temple of Hadad they constructed a magnificent temple dedicated to Jupiter. The city was also given a theatre, baths, a gymnasium and a hippodrome, the exact locations of which are still not known with certainty, buried as they are under centuries of subsequent building. The population then was estimated at around 100,000, largely Semitic in ethnicity.

In the 5th and 6th centuries under the Byzantines, Damascus was made to suffer for its religious beliefs and its

Images of Paradise on the Treasury of the Great Umayyad Mosque

inhabitants were condemned by Constantinople as Monophysites, since they believed in Christ's divine nature, as opposed to the Orthodox view that Christ's nature was both human and divine. Heretics were thrown in jail and many were massacred or had a fiscal tax imposed on them, so when the Muslim armies arrived, they were greeted as liberators. The son of the Christian who handed over the city to the Muslims himself became the chief army minister, and many Christians went on to serve in the army which subsequently established a Muslim empire stretching from the Atlantic to the Indus. Today the Christian element in the population is around ten per cent, and many continue to serve at high levels in government and the professions.

There is no religious discrimination in Syria, and often the only clue to someone's Christian origins is their name, Daoud for men or Sawsan for women, for example.

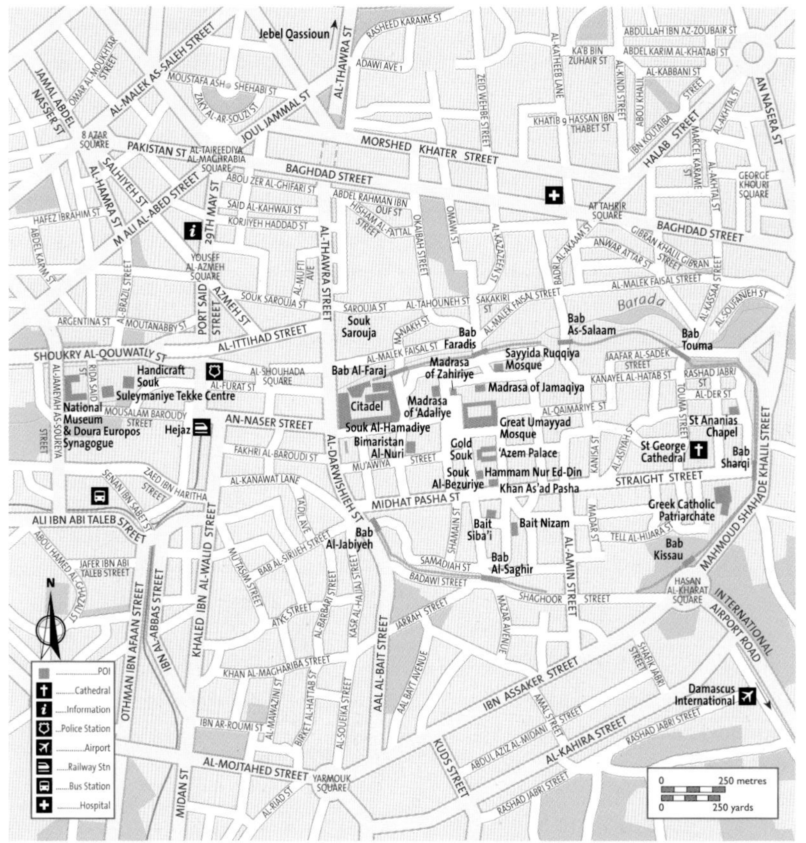

Great Umayyad Mosque

Ranking alongside Jerusalem's Dome of the Rock as one of the most holy shrines of early Islam, the Umayyad Mosque is the single most remarkable building in Syria. Originally a pagan temple to Hadad, local Semitic god of storms, the Romans reused the site to build a colossal temple to Jupiter, one of the biggest Roman sanctuaries of the East. With the advent of Christianity the temple was converted to a magnificent cathedral dedicated to St John the Baptist, whose tomb still lies within what is now the prayer hall of the mosque.

The tourist (non-Muslim) entrance is on the north side of the mosque, after the 'Putting on special clothes room', and past Saladin's tomb which warrants a brief detour to admire the 17th-century Damascus tilework.

Open: 9am–5pm. Admission charge includes a woman's full-length gown and a short pamphlet on the mosque. Shoes must be shed before entering the courtyard and men should be in long trousers, though short-sleeved shirts are acceptable.

Minarets

The three huge minarets of the mosque are taller and more imposing than any others in the Old City. The tallest is the Tower of Jesus, in the southeast corner opposite Laila's Restaurant, from where Muslim tradition holds that the Prophet Jesus will descend on the Day of Judgement to fight the Antichrist.

EARLY HARMONY

For the first 70 years or so after the Arab conquest in 636, the mosque continued to be used by Christians as well as Muslims, who shared the space, orienting their prayers towards their respective spiritual homes, south towards Mecca or west towards Rome. Caliph Walid I then decided, as the Muslim population grew, that a large congregational mosque was required to accommodate the entire community, and negotiated the departure of the Christians in exchange for four other sites in the Old City where churches were to be erected. The mosque took seven years to build, 708–15, and exhausted the state revenue.

Courtyard and mosaics

The vast courtyard is dazzling with its white paving, but take time to admire the stunning 8th-century green and gold mosaics, executed by Syrian and Byzantine craftsmen, representing paradise with rivers and trees. The finest is 30m (98ft) long, in the sheltered western portico.

Prayer hall

You can enter and sit here on the carpets, enjoying the calm and peaceful atmosphere and working out the elements of what was once the Cathedral of St John. Note the four *mihrabs*, or prayer niches, in the south wall, each used by the four different schools of Islamic law.

Exterior walls

As you leave the mosque, make a point of observing the exterior walls to see the layers of construction. The massive limestone blocks of the lower parts are unmistakeably Roman, being the foundations of the Temple of Jupiter, and on the south wall opposite the craft shops look out for the elaborate lintel with a Greek inscription above the blocked-up gate. This was the shared Muslim and Christian entrance (*see panel opposite*). Notice, too, the step-pyramid-like architectural decoration along the top of the eastern wall; known as *merlons*, these are a Babylonian feature.

The magnificent Great Umayyad Mosque stands in the heart of Old Damascus

The Muslim Quarter

In terms of area, the Muslim Quarter accounts for around 60 per cent of the total 3sq km (1¼sq miles) within the walls, the Jewish Quarter around 15 per cent, and the Christian Quarter around 25 per cent. Distances are therefore relatively small between the major monuments described below.

Bimaristan Al-Nuri

Arguably the most fascinating place to visit after the Great Umayyad Mosque, this 12th-century hospital was the most advanced medical institution of its time, and has now been converted to the Museum of Arab Science and Medicine. Consisting of three halls set round a courtyard, the museum gives an excellent introduction to the early Arab scientists, explaining their discoveries and inventions. One hall is dedicated to herbs and their properties, widely used in the Arab world long before they became popular in the West. Another displays complex and advanced dental instruments and other surgical instruments for circumcision, and explains the virtues of good hygiene, baths and the detoxification process.
Open: 8am–2pm. Closed: Tue. Admission charge.

Citadel

This powerfully built structure is deceptively vast, built as it is on flat ground beside the Barada River in the northwest corner of the walled Old City. It dates mainly from Saladin's

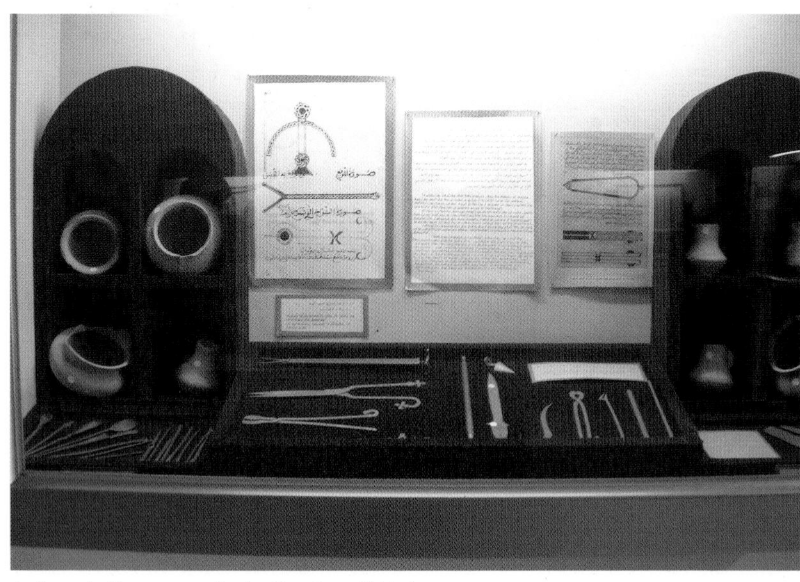

Arab surgical instruments in the Bimaristan Al-Nuri

Ayyubid dynasty in the 13th century and was attacked by the Crusaders three times. Badly damaged during the Mongol invasions later that century, it was then rebuilt by the Ottoman Turks who continued to use it as a military base for five centuries.
Al-Thawra St. Open: 10am–noon. Admission charge.

Madrasa of 'Adaliye and Zahiriye
These two fine madrasa (religious schools) lie opposite each other just north of the Souk Al-Hamadiye near the Umayyad Mosque. Both date from the 13th century and one contains the tomb of Al-'Adil, one of Saladin's brothers, the other the tomb of Baibars (whose epithet was Al-Zahir), the famous Mameluke Sultan.
His tomb chamber is finely decorated with green and gold mosaics, reminiscent of those in the Umayyad Mosque.
Open: 8am–2pm. Admission by tip to the guardian.

Madrasa of Jamaqiya
This late 15th-century Mameluke madrasa has now been converted into a museum of Arabic calligraphy and epigraphy (inscriptions). Apart from the exhibits of illuminated Korans and explanations about early Arabic script, the building itself is beautifully decorated with fine stained-glass windows and a pretty fountain.
Open: 8am–2pm. Closed: Tue. Admission charge.

The inner recesses of the citadel

Sayyida Ruqqiya Mosque
This modern Shi'a mosque is built in the Iranian style and lies in the Shi'a district of the Old City known as Amara, in the north around Bab Al-Amara. It houses the tomb of Ruqqiya, one of the daughters of the Shi'a martyr Al-Hussein, and is thus a popular place of pilgrimage especially for women, who come in droves shrouded head to toe in their black robes, contrasting starkly with the gaudy gold decoration and brightly coloured blue and green tilework. Inside, the men's and women's areas are totally segregated. Shoes must be taken off before entering the mausoleum.
Open: 9am–6pm. Free admission, but a tip is expected for the custodian who provides the full-length gowns for women at the entrance.

Mosque architecture

Syria played a key role in the evolution of mosque architecture, and its influences can be seen on subsequent mosque design in Egypt and right across the Arab world to Muslim Spain.

When the early Muslim armies surged northwards out of the Arabian Peninsula in the early 7th century, there was no previously existing concept of how a mosque should look. The *Ka'aba* at Mecca was Islam's first monument, but it consisted merely of the holy stone which was circumambulated. At prayer times the Prophet Muhammad and his Companions had simply put a spear in the ground to mark the *qibla* (direction of Mecca) and prayed wherever they happened to be.

After the Prophet's death, the Umayyad Caliph Al-Walid sent skilled workmen down to extend the Mosque of the Prophet over Muhammad's grave at Medina. In Damascus, his capital, the Caliph used, albeit within the constraints of the existing Roman and Christian site, the idea of an open congregational mosque with shaded arcades round a courtyard and a prayer hall built into the *qibla* wall. He chose to lavish so much money on the construction and beautification of the Great Umayyad Mosque to make a political statement to his newly conquered Christian subjects that Islam could outdo Christianity and create a building with representations of Paradise that exceeded any previous Christian monument. The Syrian countryside would have been littered with thousands of 4th-, 5th- and 6th-

The depictions of Paradise in the Great Umayyad Mosque were created to outdo any earlier Byzantine mosaics

century Byzantine churches, and the Umayyad Mosque took its inspiration partly from such examples as St Simeon's Basilica, of which the dome and gabled façade of the Umayyad Mosque is reminiscent.

Minaret

Minarets were first used here in Damascus at the Great Umayyad Mosque, from the existing towers built at the corners of the Roman *temenos* (sacred space) enclosure. Before this, early Muslims had simply climbed on to the roof to make the call to prayer, but here, they recognised the benefit of being higher – Islam was always a practical religion. Early minarets all followed this square shape.

Mihrab

The Umayyad Mosque has the earliest extant example of a curved niche or *mihrab* to mark the *qibla*. The first ever examples are thought to have been at Medina and Jerusalem, but these do not survive today.

Decorative elements

Islam forbids the use of the human form in all decorative art, so verses of the Koran were used instead, embellished in exotic calligraphic styles, along with foliage, trees and geometric patterns to enhance the interiors of prayer halls and especially the *mihrab*, where most attention tended to be focused.

The earliest minarets evolved in Syria

Under the patronage of the Mameluke sultans from the 13th to the 16th century, much magnificent decorative art evolved, notably the famous Damascus tilework in blues, greens and black on a white background, and marquetry in both wood and marble, all used extensively in mosques around the city. A typical Mameluke pattern is the star with six points which repeats itself outwards to infinity.

Another innovation from Syria was the vaulting system of *muqarnas*, also popularly known as beehive or stalactite vaulting. Often found above *mihrabs* or in curved domes, it is where a multitude of carved niches is piled upon one another, giving a honeycomb effect, thought to symbolise the honey the believer is promised in Paradise.

Damascus palaces: 'Azem Palace, Bait Nizam and Bait Siba'i

Damascus conceals its magnificent palaces of the 18th and 19th centuries behind closed doors and high walls. From the street even the doorway is not always a clue to the opulence that lies within. In total there are well over 150, many of which have in recent years been converted to restaurants in grand style. The following are the finest to visit and all are within a few minutes of each other.

THE LAYOUT OF AN ARAB COURTYARD HOUSE

An Ottoman house traditionally had three courtyards, each with a central fountain and rooms on all four sides. From the street the first courtyard you enter is known as the *salamlik*, where the men of the house receive guests. The grander palaces will have both a summer and a winter reception room. Beyond the *salamlik*, the second and much larger courtyard is the *haramlik*, where the women of the household and the family live. This is generally the most lavishly decorated area. Finally, off the *haramlik* is the *khadamlik*, or servants' area, the smallest and simplest of the courtyards, where the kitchens and food storage would be.

'Azem Palace

Now officially the Museum of Popular Arts and Traditions, the 'Azem Palace is the largest palace in Damascus. Deceptively modest from the outside, the dog-leg entrance opens out into the first of three spacious courtyards. The highly distinguished Azem family produced no less than five governors of Damascus. Built in 1749–52, the site is thought to have been that of the Mameluke governor. During the French Mandate it was used as the French Institute, but after independence it was purchased by the government in 1951 and turned into the current museum.

The first courtyard of Bait Nizam

The rooms of the palace have been furnished as they would have been, often with mannequins enacting daily domestic scenes. The *haramlik* also contains its own intimate hammam, conveying very well how pampered the family members were. Life could be lived entirely behind closed doors, away from prying eyes and unwanted guests. The *khadamlik* now contains the administrative offices and is closed to the public.

Open: 9am–5.30pm (summer); 9am–3.30pm (winter).
Closed: Tue (all year).
Admission charge.

Bait Nizam

There are no set opening times but mornings until 2pm are a visitor's best bet, though sometimes you will find the door open even after dark. Signposted off Straight Street, the palace is occasionally used for evening functions and performances with whirling dervishes. At one stage the palace served as the residence of the British Consul; then it deteriorated while it was used as a foam factory for much of the 20th century, until it was the subject of a restoration project financed by the Agha Khan Foundation.
Free admission.

Bait Siba'i

Tucked discreetly down an unlikely side street, this fine palace is on a smaller scale than Bait Nizam and once served as the residence of the German Consul. It, too, has been carefully restored under the auspices of the Agha Khan Foundation, and there is talk that, along with Bait Nizam and the nearby Bait Quwatli, the three palaces may be converted to a luxury 5-star hotel.
Free admission.

There is superb attention to detail in the palaces

Spices on sale in the souks

Damascus souks

The souks (markets) of Damascus are concentrated within the walls of the Old City and throb with life from around 10am till around 10pm daily except Fridays. The most colourful ones are described below, and all are within a few minutes' walk of each other.

Gold Souk

Clustered partly round the 'Azem Palace and partly along Mu'awiya St, the gold shops sell every conceivable item of jewellery for women. Muslim men do not wear gold, as tradition holds that it can make them infertile, which is why their wedding rings are usually silver. If a man is wearing a gold ring he is generally a Christian. For silver jewellery, the best place to look is the Handicraft Souk near the National Museum.

Souk Al-Bezuriye

Wonderfully aromatic, this vast, high-ceilinged spice souk is definitely a place to linger. The merchants have their sacks of spices and herbs on display and you can sample freely, buying 100g (3½oz) of this and that. Scattered among the spice vendors are stalls selling the excellently soft Aleppo olive and laurel soap and perfumes, as well as a plethora of sweet stalls, offering every sticky sweetie imaginable, packaged or loose. At the far end on the left before you emerge into Straight Street, look out for the finest baths in the Old City, Hammam Nur Ed-Din, and just a few metres beyond it is the entrance to Khan As'ad Pasha, the city's largest *khan*.

Souk Al-Hamadiye

Arguably the most dramatic and visually imposing souk anywhere in the

Middle East, the sheer scale and height of space enclosed by its vast tunnel roof of corrugated iron will make you feel dwarfed. Many of the stalls have upstairs shops as well, and yet there is a great sense of space above, the bullet-holed roof from fighting during the French Mandate in the 1920s letting in specks of light like stars in the dark firmament. It runs for a full 500m (550yds) and has a width of at least 15m (16yds), its shops selling everything from clothes, shoes and handbags to towels, Korans and stuffed animals. No motorised vehicles are permitted, but bicycles weave their way in between the pedestrians. You could spend a whole day here, exploring and poking down the side alleys, and still not get to grips with it.

Additional local colour is provided by water sellers and tamarind juice sellers, pouring their products from magnificent gold or silver long-spouted ewers into tiny glasses for a token handful of Syrian pounds. Always take your time strolling along this magnificent walkway, and enjoy particularly the moment when you emerge into the Roman colonnade by the open square in front of the Umayyad Mosque, its Corinthian columns often draped in carpets for sale.

Souk Sarouja

Just outside the Old City walls by the citadel but on the other side of the Barada River, this colourful, old-fashioned souk sells material for tents and awnings, has superb cobblers, and sells leather goods and hardware from nuts and bolts to wonderful handmade wooden ladders.

The souks sell all sorts of wares

Walk: Damascus Old City

This walk serves as an introduction to the major Muslim monuments of the Old City. Mornings are the best time to go, between 9am and 2pm, standard opening hours. Avoid Tuesdays, when the 'Azem Palace is shut.

Allow a good three to four hours, including visiting times. The total distance is about 3km (2 miles).

Start at the citadel entrance beside the Saladin statue on Al-Thawra St.

1 The Citadel

After many years of restoration, the huge and powerfully built citadel is now open from 10am until noon. It dates mostly from the 13th century and was in use until 1985 as a prison.

Turn left as you leave the citadel and continue for 150m (164yds) along Al-Thawra St till you reach the entrance to Souk Al-Hamadiye.

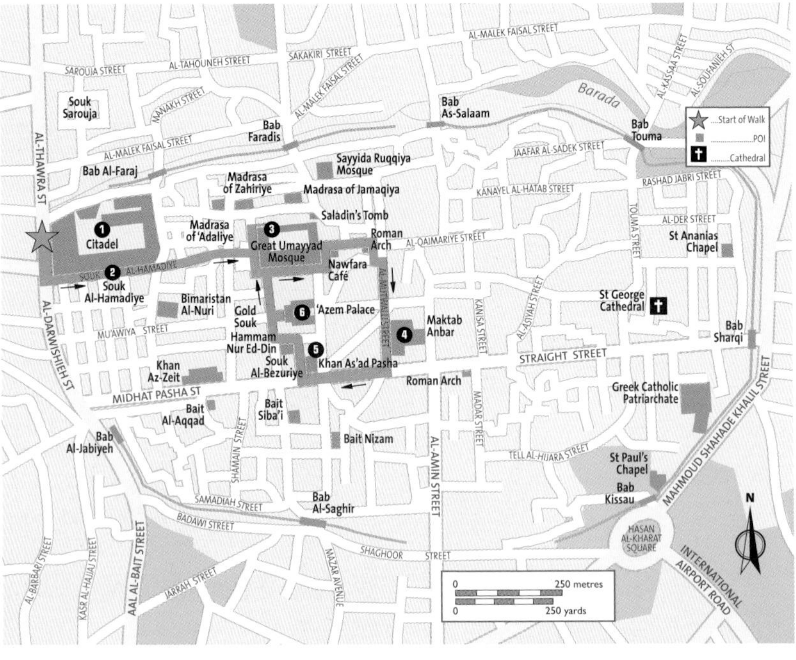

2 Souk Al-Hamadiye

This magnificent Ottoman souk with its high, arched corrugated iron roof runs for 500m (550yds) along the course of what was once the approach to the Roman temple of Jupiter. The double-storeyed shops sell everything from ice cream to exotic clothing, carpets to underwear.

Follow the souk till you emerge past the remnants of the Roman colonnade into the open square in front of the mosque, and go to the tourist entrance in the side alley to the left where the entry fee is paid and gowns collected for women.

3 Great Umayyad Mosque

Emerging from the ticket office, you pass Saladin's tomb on your left with its reddish ribbed dome, before entering the mosque courtyard (*see pp32–3*).

On leaving the mosque through the same gate, re-enter the open square and follow the walls round to the left and left again past the shops to get to the rear (east) wall. Steps here lead down to the famous Nawfara Café where you can stop; then continue along Al-Qaimariye St to the Roman arch, then turning right into Al-Mutwalli St to reach Maktab Anbar on your left after some 200m (220yds).

4 Maktab Anbar

This 19th-century palace is the headquarters of the Old Damascus Directorate, where all restoration plans for the Old City are administered and coordinated. You can wander in and stroll round the three courtyards.

Continue south for another 100m (110yds) till you reach the crossroads with Straight Street and turn right, continuing for some 350m (380yds) until you reach the Souk Al-Bezuriye (Spice Market) entrance on your right, a high-roofed cobbled street.

5 Khan As'ad Pasha

Just 50m (55yds) into the souk on the right stands the massive entrance to this, Damascus' largest *khan* (caravanserai) with nine domes and fine black and white stonework.

Continue a further 100m (110yds) till the souk opens up into a little square; the entrance to 'Azem Palace is on the right.

6 'Azem Palace

This outstanding Ottoman complex is where the governors of the city used to reside, its courtyards now a museum.

Turn right to retrace your steps back into the square in front of the mosque and out through the Souk Al-Hamadiye.

In the Souk Al-Hamadiye

The Christian Quarter and its churches

Wandering the streets of the Christian Quarter, set within the northeast section of the walled Old City, you will notice a different feel to the Muslim and Jewish Quarters, richer, and a little more sophisticated in its shops and restaurants. Alcohol is served freely and sold in the shops here, and the residents, especially the women, are dressed in more Western styles, with even the older women in skirts and short-sleeved tops and without head coverings. The two gates leading into the Christian Quarter are Bab Touma and Bab Sharqi, and the main street is Touma St, running north-south to reach Straight Street. Scattered about in the quarter are some ten churches belonging to various denominations.

Greek Catholic Patriarchate

By far the grandest of Damascus' churches, with imposing basalt columns and icons, this fine church welcomes visitors to join its services. It forms the centre of a complex (with a school, monastery and bookshop) whose head is the Melkite Patriarch of Antioch. Set behind high railings, its distinctive clock and bell tower plays its own tune.
Free admission.

St Ananias Chapel

This most memorable and famous of the Christian sites in Damascus was the original house of St Ananias, who converted St Paul to Christianity. Now a chapel with a tangibly pious atmosphere, it is entered by descending 23 ancient basalt steps leading down to what was street level in the time of Christ. After the Muslim conquest in 636 the chapel was used as a place of worship by both Muslims and Christians, with a *mihrab* (prayer niche) in the south wall, and an apse to the east. Even into Ottoman times the Turks maintained oil lamps burning day and night. In the late 19th century the Franciscans took custody and converted the building into a chapel, restoring it to its present form in 1973.

Note how the three-scene altarpiece follows the Arabic right-to-left sequence, showing, far right, Paul falling from his horse as God appears to him in a flash of light, in the centre,

CONVERSION OF ST PAUL

Originally called Saul, he was trained as a Pharisee and was actively involved in rounding up Christians to arrest them. As he rode towards Damascus, he was blinded by a light from heaven and a voice cried out, 'Saul, Saul, why are you persecuting me?' He was led into the city where he was met by a local Christian, Ananias, who gave him shelter and converted him, whereupon his sight returned. Renamed Paul, he fled the city at a spot now marked by St Paul's Chapel at Bab Kissan, and spent the remainder of his life travelling throughout the eastern Mediterranean, building a network of churches and preaching to the Gentiles. He thus became the founder of Christianity, turning it from a small sect into a world religion.

Ananias leading Paul and restoring his sight, and left, Paul being lowered over the city walls in a basket to escape. The chapel is still in use as a place of worship and a marble basin set into the wall carries holy water. There is also a souvenir shop.

Open: 9am–6pm. Free admission.

Courtyard of St Ananias Chapel

Syrian inventions

Far too little is known, and even less written about, the discoveries and inventions which originated in this part of the Arab world, and which we in the West generally assume came from the Greeks. Here are just a few of the more significant ones.

Dentistry and anaesthetics

The Arab dentist Al-Zahrawi, who died in 1013, used gold and silver fillings, only resorting to extraction in extremis. Arabs were also the inventors of the first anaesthetics, in the form of alcohol mixed with hashish, opium and belladonna, soaked in a sponge and held to the nose.

Globes and maps

Many Muslim scholars knew by the 9th century that the earth was a sphere, 500 years before Galileo. Early Muslim astronomers' calculations of the earth's circumference were a mere 200km (124 miles) adrift. The first ever globe was taken by the geography scholar Al-Idrisi to the court of King Roger of Sicily in the 12th century, and he also produced the first map of the world, remarkably accurately.

Maths and numerals

The first ever numerals appeared in print around 835 in the works of the Muslim mathematicians Al-Khawarizmi and Al-Kindi. Algebra is an Arabic word, and algorithms and trigonometry originated here, imported into Europe a good 300 years later through Latin translations. Al-Kindi also discovered frequency analysis, thereby creating the basis for modern cryptology and enabling all the codes of the ancient world to be solved.

Medicine and pharmacy

Arab scientists were the founders of pharmacy and over 80 medical words have been taken from Arabic into European languages. They made anti-toxins from plant extracts and potions for constipation, jaundice and migraines. Dried lizard was used as an aphrodisiac, and today stalls can still be seen in Old Damascus selling various dried parts of animals' anatomy as medical cures for a variety of ailments.

Indeed, the modern trend for natural remedies was the norm in the Arab world long ago; aromatherapy was first documented in the 13th century. Myrrh was used as an antiseptic for diarrhoea and for skin diseases, while rose water was advised to help with headaches and palpitations and to regain consciousness after fainting. The properties of garlic were recorded as generally antiseptic, anti-flu, anti-cancer and anti-high blood pressure. Valerium was used to calm nervous illnesses, pourpier to activate the memory and tone the nervous centres, while tamarind was a gentle laxative and parsley a diuretic.

Other inventions

Many Arab lifestyle inventions were taken back to Europe by returning Crusaders, such as soap and shampoo (novelties to the unwashed Franks), quilted bedding and carpets. The list also includes the camera (from Arabic *qamara*, meaning dark or private room) and the fountain pen, and many, many more.

In addition, the Arabic word '*saqq*' is the origin of our word cheque, and existed in the 9th century, meaning a written vow to pay for goods when delivered, so as to avoid the danger of having cash stolen when crossing dangerous terrain. Hence a Muslim businessman was able to cash a cheque in China drawn on his bank in Baghdad over 1,200 years ago.

Shops in Old Damascus still sell ingredients for curious herbal remedies

The National Museum

This pleasant and manageably sized museum houses Syria's top treasures, set within a purpose-built modern site and surrounded by an attractively laid-out garden scattered with architectural fragments not quite up to the standard to be displayed inside. Allow about one and a half to two hours for a complete visit, focusing especially on the highlights described below. Afterwards enjoy a drink or a light sandwich at the museum's garden café and a browse in the bookshop, which also sells souvenirs. No photography is allowed inside the museum.
Open: Wed, Thur & Sat–Mon 9am–6pm, Fri 9am–12.30pm & 2–6pm (summer); Wed, Thur & Sat–Mon 9am–4pm, Fri 9am–12.30pm & 2–4pm (winter). Closed: Tue. Admission charge.

Doura Europos Synagogue

Located at the extreme left end of the museum, behind a door across an open courtyard often kept locked by the guardian, this synagogue is the original building, dismantled piece by piece and reconstructed here. It owes its remarkable state of preservation and the strength of the wall colours to the fact that the synagogue was found in 1932 at Doura Europos on the banks of the Euphrates completely filled up with dry earth.

Most remarkable of all, however, is that the scenes from the Old Testament depicted on the walls show the patriarchs and prophets in human form, in defiance of Talmudic tradition. The frescoes date to the 2nd century, when the local Jews would have been strongly Hellenised. Those on the Torah wall are clearest, depicting a cycle of tableaux at four heights, including Moses as a baby in four scenes being rescued from the bulrushes, Moses parting the waters of the Red Sea in the exodus from Egypt, and the Egyptians being drowned.

Hypogeum of Yarhai

In the same hall from where the synagogue is approached, steps lead down into the reconstructed underground tomb (hypogeum) of Yarhai, brought here from Palmyra in 1934 and painstakingly reassembled block by block. For anyone not able to get to Palmyra in person, this tomb gives an excellent idea of the opulence of the burial chambers in the Valley of Tombs. Built of impressive white limestone from the local Palmyra quarry, even the doors are crafted to look like wood. There are three chambers and to the left the late Yarhai presides over his own funeral banquet in Roman style, the niches full of statue busts of deceased members of the family looking on.

Mari

The most memorable of the displays from the Mari site are the stylised statues of the king, head shaven with long beard, dressed only in the typical puffy skirt of sheep's wool. Do not miss the spectacular cylinder seal of an eagle with lion's head, the wings and body made from lapis lazuli, the head and tail of gold leaf.

Mosaics

To the left as you enter the museum is the Classical Antiquity wing, in which the mosaics from the south around Bosra are particularly impressive. They were lifted out in their entirety from the Roman villas where they were found. Dating to the 3rd and 4th centuries, they are fine allegories with women representing Earth, Justice and Philosophy.

Ugarit

The exceptional, finely crafted ivory work is the chief exhibit in the displays from the Ugarit site, along with some of the famous clay tablets written in the Phoenician alphabet, from which our own alphabet developed.

The façade of the National Museum with rescued elements of the palace Qasr Al-Hayr Al-Gharbi

South of Damascus

Located 140km (87 miles) south of Damascus at the surprisingly high altitude of 800m (2,625ft), Bosra is the major site in the south of Syria, and, after Palmyra, the country's most important Roman site. It can be visited as a fairly lengthy day trip from Damascus. Its extraordinary theatre, concealed within an Ayyubid fort and remarkably well preserved, has been awarded UNESCO World Heritage status, and ranks alongside Aspendos in southern Turkey and Leptis Magna in Libya in size and scale.

Bosra

What makes the whole Roman city of Bosra so distinctive as a site is the blackness of all the buildings, shaped from the volcanic local basalt, so different to the white limestone and marble generally associated with classical sites.

There's a simple café on site.

Theatre

One of the first major monuments to be restored since independence in 1946, the theatre at Bosra has survived earthquakes and invasions, the latter thanks to its conversion by Saladin's Ayyubid dynasty to a fort, making it completely invisible from the outside. Only once inside the fortifications do you see for the first time the astonishing Roman theatre, its seating virtually complete to its 37 rows. The stage building, too, is magnificently preserved, with much fine detail and carving. The seating capacity was 15,000, and during the Bosra Festival in early September at least that number crams inside to enjoy the dancing, drama and music.

Open: 9am–6pm (summer); 9am–4pm (winter). Admission charge.

Town

The remainder of the town can be viewed from the tower of the fort/theatre, but it's also well worth taking a leisurely stroll about the site.

THE VOLCANIC HAURAN REGION

The rather bleak landscape in this part of southwestern Syria is scattered with obvious signs of relatively recent volcanic activity, including many extinct volcanic cones. Some have been used defensively as the sites of forts such as Salkhad and even the Arab castle at Palmyra. The lava from these cones solidified to form the distinctive black basalt of the region, used in many buildings first by the Romans, then the Byzantines. In Mameluke 13th-century times, it was used in the style known as ablaq, where it was alternated with white limestone in bands to great effect.

In the 19th century, following the Druze/Christian conflicts, thousands of Druze took refuge here, only recently cleared out by the authorities. In the town you can visit the fine, late 2nd-century baths, a public amenity free to all and used daily by most inhabitants. Besides the huge Roman reservoir, 120m by 150m (390ft by 490ft), known locally as Pool of the Pilgrimage (Birkat Al-Hajj) where the pilgrim caravan en route to Mecca used to stop for water, the other main buildings to look out for are the basilica and several early mosques built mainly in 13th-century Ayyubid times when Bosra was an outpost guarding the southern approaches to Damascus. It was in the basilica here that the monk Bahira was said to have met Muhammad, who was leading a trading caravan from Mecca before the Koran was revealed to him, and predicted his extraordinary future. *Open unfenced site. Free admission.*

The Roman theatre at Bosra is thought to be the best-preserved in the world

Drive: South of Damascus

The reward of this drive is an enjoyable and varied excursion, encompassing early churches, Roman mosaics, the large Roman site of Bosra and Islamic castles and mosques from the time of Saladin.

A full day should be allowed, with about four hours' driving and around four hours' sightseeing. It is preferable to spend a night at Bosra in the Cham Hotel, but most visitors do this as a day trip, hiring a car with or without a driver. The total distance is about 350km (217 miles).

Start in Damascus. Take the fastest route south on the dual carriageway towards the Jordanian border for about 80km (50 miles), then take the exit for Ezraa. In Ezraa, follow the fork off the main road left towards the 'Archaeological Area' for about 2km (1¼ miles).

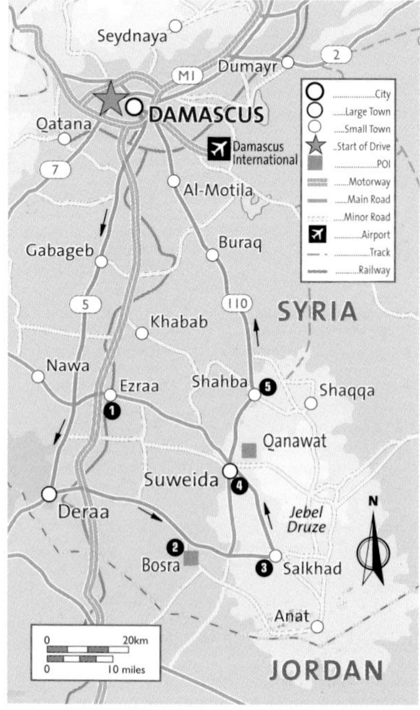

1 Ezraa

In this unlikely spot lies the Greek Orthodox church of St George, dated from its lintel to 515, one of the earliest churches in Syria still in use.

Return to the dual carriageway south and continue to the Deraa exit, forking left (east) to Bosra.

2 Bosra

It's a good idea to have lunch here, so you can linger longest at this major Roman site, and really make the most of enjoying the fort/theatre and the extensive ruins of the town behind (*see pp50–51*).

Head east now on the Suweida road and follow the signs to Salkhad, 29km (18 miles) from Bosra, heading straight up to the castle.

ST GEORGE

That the English patron saint should be buried here is yet another of Syria's little surprises. Thought to have been a soldier martyred in Palestine in AD 303 for his Christian beliefs, many myths began to accumulate around him including those of fighting the dragon to convert the townspeople to Christianity. All over the region there are many churches and even monasteries named after him. In England he did not become the patron saint until the 14th century, invoked as protector of the army and the kingdom.

3 Salkhad

Set on its unmistakeable volcanic cone, the crumbling fortress of Salkhad dates from 1277 and completely dominates the surrounding landscape. The town below also boasts a fine 13th-century minaret standing 12m (39ft) tall.

Head north on the road to Suweida. These roads are usually very empty.

4 Suweida

The museum is signposted off the main road and warrants a half-hour stop to look at the very fine 3rd-century mosaics found in Roman villas locally.

Open: 9am–6pm (summer); 9am–4pm (winter). Closed: Tue (all year).

Continue north for 16km (10 miles) to reach the town of Shahba.

5 Shahba

Dispersed around the centre of the modern town is a range of unusual Roman relics of the town of Philippopolis, birthplace of Emperor Philip, on which he lavished much attention. As well as the museum with mosaics, look out for the nearby baths, the theatre and the fine forum complete with temple.

From Shahba continue north to Damascus on the slower but more direct road.

Mosaic of Neptune found near Suweida

The Druze

The base of the Druze religious community in Syria received its name of Jebel Druze, the Mountain of the Druze, under the French Mandate. It had formerly been known as Jebel Al-Arab, the Mountain of the Arabs. Like so many persecuted minorities, the Druze have tended to take refuge in mountains, away from the ruling authorities, where they can be left in peace to pursue their beliefs. Originally an esoteric offshoot of the Shi'a Ismai'ili sect of Islam dating from the 10th century, they are now regarded as heretics by both Sunni and Shi'a sects.

The Druze village of Mushannaf

The religion itself is a complex mix of neo-Platonism, Sufi mysticism and Iranian religious tradition, and sees itself as a synthesis of the best elements of previous religions and their spiritual and social concepts.

Since 1043 it has been forbidden to convert to or from the Druze religion, so it is only possible to be born into it. It is also forbidden to marry outside it, making the Druze a very closed society in Syria, shrouded with secrecy, and rife with speculation by outsiders.

Beliefs

Druze believe in reincarnation and that everything is preordained and part of God's plan. Each soul is

GOD AS CALIPH

Founded by a Turkish preacher named Ad-Darazi, the Druze believe that the Fatimid Caliph Al-Hakim was a divine representation of God. An enigmatic figure with blue eyes, he 'disappeared' from human sight in 1021, aged 25, but was expected to return at some later point to initiate a golden age. The expectation was not unsurprising, as the Isma'ilis believed that their imams (religious leaders) were embodiments of God. However, Al-Hakim was renowned for his persecution of Jews and Christians, so the likelihood is that he was in fact murdered.

Snow lying in a Jebel Druze village

thought to come back in a new body to keep improving itself. God's fairness and justice is absolute. They reject all the Five Pillars of Islam and do not fast in Ramadan or make the pilgrimage to Mecca. Their holy day is Thursday and their chief prophet is Jethro, father-in-law to Moses. Islam's three most important prophets, Muhammad, Jesus and Moses, are all revered. The Koran and the Bible are considered sacred texts but the Druze also have their own religious texts. Instead of using mosques, they pray in ordinary, simple buildings called *khalwas* located on the edge of their villages.

Persecution and massacre

In the mid-19th century, clashes broke out between the Druze and the Maronite Christians in Lebanon, culminating in the massacre of 1860, when 11,000 Christians were killed by the Druze, with some 150 Christian villages being burnt. To this day, the Druze are known to have a strong tendency to revolt against authority and are considered fearless fighters.
In 1944 they agreed to surrender their autonomy, having been given an autonomous state in the Jebel Druze under the French Mandate.
Worldwide, the Druze community numbers something over a million, mainly concentrated in Syria and Lebanon, Jordan and Israel. Small communities also exist in Europe, Australia and the Americas.
You can investigate further online (*see www.druze.com, or www.druze.net*).

North of Damascus

Within easy striking distance of Damascus to the north (see pp58–9 for driving directions) are a number of interesting Christian sites all set in the Qalamoun Mountains of which the following are the most worth visiting. They are all open sites with free admission.

Maaloula

Set in a cleft of the Qalamoun Mountains 53km (33 miles) north of Damascus, Maaloula is known above all as one of the Christian villages where Aramaic is still in use. It also has two functioning monasteries.

Mar Sarkis

Perched dramatically at the top of the gorge beside the Maaloula Hotel, directly above and overlooking the village of Maaloula, this ancient monastery is probably Syria's most interesting in architectural terms. The church is divided into three aisles and the altar has been dated, along with the wood in the beams, as being 2,000 years old. Among its many fine icons is an early John the Baptist complete with sheep and serpent. The monastery makes its own wine and *araq*, and offers sample tasters from its excellent little shop.

ARAMAIC

The language of Christ sounds similar to modern Arabic and Hebrew in its phonetics and gutturals. The attendants at Mar Sarkis will happily give you a rendition of the Lord's Prayer in Aramaic, used today only in liturgy, not in everyday speech.

Mar Thekla

From Mar Sarkis you should make a point of walking the 15 minutes or so past the Maaloula Hotel along the road and down the hill into the gorge of St Thekla, said to have opened up to enable her to flee her persecutors. The narrow defile winds impressively down towards the town, emerging beside the Mar Thekla monastery, famous for its grotto where St Thekla is said to have sheltered, and now credited with the power to cure illnesses and perform miracles. Inside the monastery church, look out for the famous icon of Jacob's Ladder, with black imp-like devils pulling their victims off into hellfire.

Mar Mousa

This remarkable desert monastery clinging to the cliff face an hour's drive north of Damascus is unique in the region, in that its express purpose is the bringing together of Muslims and Christians. Father Paolo, a Jesuit priest, came here in 1988 and saw it as his mission to rescue the monastery from a derelict shell, and through ten years of sheer drive and energy, restored it to a living community. Muslims are welcome to join in Mass, as are all other Christian denominations. The church has fine 11th-century frescoes, notably of the Last Judgement and Adam and Eve. The monastery offers basic overnight accommodation and a simple evening meal and breakfast, but should only be visited in a respectful frame of mind by those genuinely interested in the furtherance of the monastery's aims. Avoid Fridays when the monastery's meagre resources are overrun with local visitors, including many Iraqi refugees. Water is especially limited and overnight visitors should not expect to take showers.

There is an excellent shop, from which it is a 10- to 15-minute walk up the series of steps to the monastery entrance, through a low door to the left.

Open for day visitors until 6pm.

Mar Sarkis at Maaloula

Drive: North of Damascus

This drive takes you into the foothills of the Qalamoun Mountains, the stronghold of Christianity in Syria, to visit a range of churches and monasteries.

It will take a full day. However, if you want to extend it and are seriously interested in these Eastern Christian communities, you could stay at the monastery of Mar Mousa. The total distance is about 250km (155 miles).

Start in Damascus. Set off north, initially on the main road to Aleppo, then fork left towards Seydnaya and Maaloula, reaching Seydnaya after 26km (16 miles).

1 Seydnaya

At an altitude of 1,650m (5,400ft) and set slightly above the town you will find the Greek Orthodox Convent of Our Lady of Seydnaya. After Jerusalem this is the second-holiest site of pilgrimage for Greek Orthodox Christians, thanks to its icon of the Virgin Mary, said to have been painted by St Luke. During the Crusades the Knights Templar came here to collect oil that supposedly oozed from it as a holy relic.

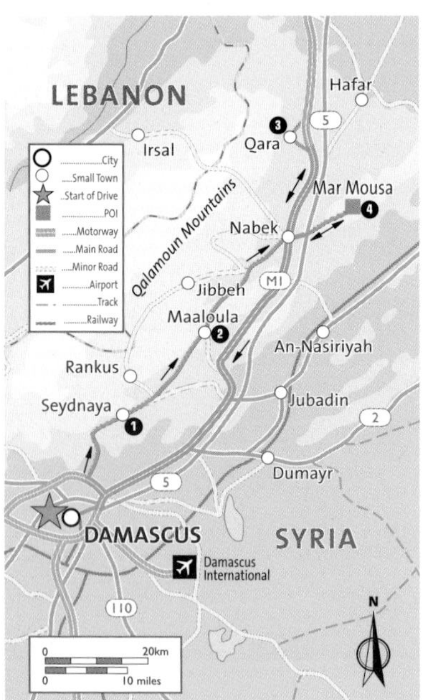

From Seydnaya you now continue another 27km (17 miles) north to reach the town of Maaloula, driving through the town and forking left at the roundabout to Mar Sarkis, which you will see perched on top of the rock overlooking the town.

2 Maaloula

Begin by visiting the monastery of Mar Sarkis above the town (*see p56*), making sure to stop at their well-stocked shop, before walking down to visit the Mar Thekla monastery at the top of the town through the defile (*see p56*). Maaloula is the best place for lunch, with a choice of places either up round Mar Sarkis or down in the town.

From Maaloula drive on north some 35km (22 miles) to reach the town of Qara, just west of the main Aleppo highway.

3 Qara

In the centre of town ask for the Great Mosque (Al-Jaami' Al-Kabeer). Originally the Cathedral of St Nicholas, it was converted to a mosque in 1266 and boasts a very fine façade. Beyond the town, 1km ($^2/_3$ mile) west towards the mountains, you can drive to visit the Convent of St Jacques, built on the foundations of a Roman fort and considered by experts to be the oldest in the region. One of the sisters will show you round. Visit their excellent shop if you want to buy some local produce or even jewellery.

From Qara return 16km (10 miles) to Nabek on the main Aleppo highway, then follow the signs to Mar Mousa, 15km (9 miles) away along its own tarmac road east into the desert.

4 Mar Mousa

The road now comes right to the foot of the monastery, leaving just an ascent of some 350 steps to reach the entrance. The shop is also here by the car park and there are plans to build a museum beside it, away from the monastery itself (*see p57*).

From Mar Mousa it is 94km (58 miles) back to Damascus by the direct route, returning to Nabek then heading south on the main highway.

The gorge of St Thekla

Arab Christianity

Many Westerners assume that all Arabs are Muslims, so are surprised to discover that ten per cent of Syria's population are Arab Christians. True to its philosophy of peaceful co-existence between religious groupings, Syria's Ba'ath Party is totally secular with no discrimination based on religion, which is regarded as a personal matter. There are Christians at all levels in Syrian society and in the workplace, both in government and across the professions and the world of commerce. The Syrian constitution even stipulates that three government ministers must be Christian.

Christianity in the Koran

In the Koran, Christians are referred to as 'People of the Book' and it is acknowledged that Christians, Jews and Muslims are all worshipping the same One God, be he called God, Allah or Jehovah. The Koran singles out the Christians as the closest to Islam:

'You will discover that those who are most implacable in their hatred of the Muslims are the Jews and the pagans, while those nearest to them in affection are those who profess to be Christians. That is because there are priests and monks among them, and they are free of pride.'
Sura 5:85

Islam's criticism of Christianity is for its worship of the Trinity, three gods instead of one, and it strenuously denies that Jesus is the Son of God:

'Say: He is God – One!
Good – the eternally sought after!
He did not have a son
And was no one's son.'
Sura 112

Early divisions of the church

Early Christianity was accompanied by centuries of serious divisions and rivalries as bishops disagreed about various interpretations of the Bible. Disputes raged about the nature of Christ, about whether he was human or divine or both. From 325 onwards, when the Christian Emperor Constantine convened the Council of Nicaea, these arguments produced the Orthodox view that the three elements of Father, Son and Holy Ghost were equal and that Christ had a dual nature (human and divine), as opposed to both the Arian view that

Sixth-century frescoes at the Church of St Elian in Homs

the Father came before the Son and Holy Ghost, and the Monophysite view that Christ's nature was divine. Syria's Christians are mainly Monophysites, belonging to what is known as the Jacobite Church. The splintering of the faith into such schisms helped pave the way for the rapid spread of Islam across the region.

From the start, on their arrival at the gates of Damascus in 636, the Muslims displayed great tolerance toward the indigenous Christian population. They established their camp at the edge of the city and were content to build a modest place of prayer beside the Cathedral of St John which had been built under Theodosius (379–95).

Only at the beginning of the 8th century under Caliph Walid I (705–15) did things begin to change. All administrative documentation, previously in Greek or Persian, was now in Arabic, and the role of the élite Christians declined. Walid negotiated for the Christians to leave the cathedral in exchange for four sites for churches elsewhere in the Old City, and began work on the Great Umayyad Mosque, employing many Christian Byzantine masons and mosaicists.

Palmyra and beyond

Known as the Badia, the stretches of semi-desert and mountains to the east of Palmyra are the territory of Syria's nomadic Bedouin, an ever-diminishing sector of the Syrian population. More than half of Syria qualifies as Badia or steppe-land, with an annual rainfall of under 200mm (7¾in). Such land is, however, good for seasonal grazing and is home to most of Syria's sheep, goats and camels. Efforts are now in place to avoid overgrazing, with hundreds of thousands of seedlings being planted to restore damaged areas.

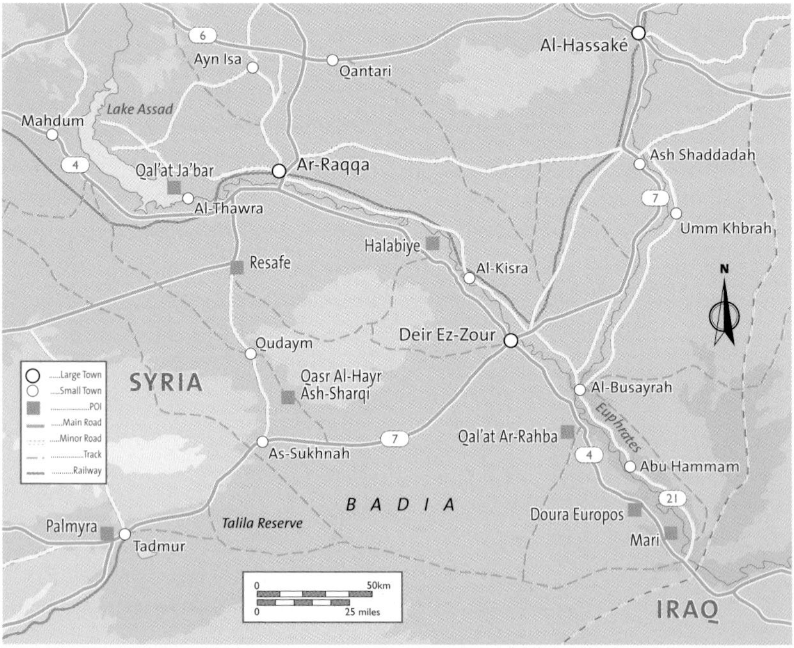

There are thought to be a million or so Bedouin in Syria, of whom some 60 per cent are thought to be fully migratory, living in tents and moving their flocks between pasture areas. Many of them are illiterate, but as more and more of them are being encouraged to settle, the Bedouin traditions are gradually breaking down. The supreme virtue of the Bedouin, *sabr*, tenacity and endurance in the face of adversity, is no longer called for. Responsibly organised tourism could play a role here in helping sustain the economic viability of the Bedouin lifestyle. Income could be supplemented through adventure holidays and camel treks, as in Jordan's Wadi Rum for example, and Bedouin handicrafts could be sold in local markets. This type of holiday, living on the edge of survival and experiencing first-hand the rigours of nature and the elements, is increasingly in demand now as a contrast to Western, comfort-based lives, and helps visitors to regain a perspective on the essentials of life.

Set in the middle of this desert, three hours' drive from Damascus, lies one of the world's most complete and evocative sites, the Roman caravan city of Palmyra, set on the edge of a massive desert oasis and guarded by an impressive Arab fort that sits astride an extinct volcano. Spend at least one night here, so you can view the ruins at sunset and at dawn when the light is at its most magical.

Running through this northeastern corner of Syria is the Euphrates, one of the great rivers of the Middle East. Along its banks the earliest civilisations grew up, and the relics of these can be seen today at the early Bronze Age site of Mari and at the Hellenistic and Roman sites of Doura Europos (*see pp72–4*).

The Arab castle that guards Palmyra

PALMYRA

In its majestic desert setting protected to the north by a range of mountains reaching 900m (2,950ft), Palmyra itself lies at a surprisingly high altitude of 600m (1,970ft), shielded to the south by its vast oasis of palm trees fed by numerous springs. Reflecting its importance as Syria's premier tourist attraction, it boasts more hotels than anywhere outside Damascus, and it is vital to spend at least one night here enjoying the silence and magic of the desert.

Arab fort

Dramatically hovering above the classical site of the Roman city, especially impressive at night under illumination, the Arab fort above Palmyra is thought to have its origins in the 12th and 13th centuries. Most of what remains today, however, dates from the early 17th century, when the Druze Emir Fakhr Ed-Din Ibn Ma'an seized much of what is now Syria and Lebanon and built a string of forts to defend himself against the Ottomans. A path leads up to it from the ruins, but most visitors arrive by vehicle on the new tarmac road. Crossing the fine drawbridge, you enter into a complex of rooms where some 600 soldiers were once garrisoned.

Open: 9am–6pm (summer); 9am–4pm (winter). Admission charge.

THE OASIS

Try to have a short walk in the palmery at some point during your stay, to get a feel for the extraordinary gardens not just of palms but of olives, pomegranates and other fruits. Between September and December the dates are harvested and you will see them for sale along the roadside, all sizes and colours. The yellow ones are the smallest and cheapest, while the most expensive are the black ones. There are over 50 words in Arabic to describe dates in all stages of ripeness, colour, sweetness and size.

Archaeological Museum

A brief visit to this small museum, on the edge of the modern town of Tadmur, is best made after seeing the Roman site itself, when the exhibits will have more impact. Of particular interest are the reconstruction of the Sanctuary of Bel, the expressive faces on the carved funeral busts, and the fragments of colourful and elaborate cloth salvaged from the mummies.

Open: 8am–6pm (summer); 8am–1pm & 2–4pm (winter).
Admission charge.

Roman city

From the Monumental Arch, on the other side of the road from the Sanctuary of Bel, you can begin an exploration of the main elements of the Roman city, with all the major public buildings to be found along the colonnaded street, which runs through the heart of the city (*see pp70–71*). Camel owners lurk with their reluctant beasts in the shadow of the arch, keen that you effect this exploration by

The *cella* of the Temple of Bel

camel rather than on foot. This is likely to be the one place where you are guaranteed a camel ride in Syria, so you may well wish to take it.

The street itself is in many ways the most interesting aspect, dating to the 2nd century. A full 1.2km (¾ mile) long, it was deliberately never paved, so that camels could walk easily along it. Including the porticos on both sides together with their shop stalls, the street was an amazing 23m (75ft) wide. Many of the 10m (33ft) high columns tumbled due to earthquakes over the centuries, now re-erected by the Syrian Department of Antiquities. The plinths jutting out halfway up the columns would originally have held busts of various Palmyrene notables who paid to have themselves immortalised, only to then be sold off in the 19th century to passing souvenir hunters for a few piastres.

Open access. Free admission.

Sanctuary of Bel

The single most impressive monument at Palmyra and the most important religious 1st-century sanctuary in the entire Middle East, this enormous complex dominates the eastern end of the ancient site. It stands beside the oasis, separated from the rest of the site by the main road. Once through the ticket office entrance, the sheer scale dwarfs, and you can vividly imagine the processions of worshippers, led by their priests, heading along the sunken open passage to the left of the entrance, winding round to the altar in front of the temple, their sacrificial animals in tow. The blood was collected and mixed

A view along the colonnaded street towards the Monumental Arch

with water, then used for irrigation to improve the soil's fertility, a good example of early recycling. The meat, too, was never wasted, but cooked and eaten.

The *cella* of the temple was completed in AD 32, and an outer colonnaded portico was added later. The *cella* was used as a church in Byzantine times and converted to a mosque in the 12th century. So much is missing now, that it is worth looking at the scaled reconstruction in the town's museum to get an idea of how the whole structure would have looked. The 18m- (59ft-) tall columns would originally have been plated in gold and silver, and any statues made of bronze, all long ago melted down and traded. Even in its current state, however, the *cella* is the undoubted centrepiece of the complex. Inside, note the shrines at either end. To the left, the shrine ceiling, heavily blackened by smoke, has seven images of the gods of the planets, surrounded by the 12 signs of the zodiac. Just in front of the entrance, note the exceptionally fine carved blocks which have fallen from the architrave, depicting a sacrificial procession and the Palmyran gods. The exotic friezes fringing the entrance carry a motif of eggs symbolising fertility, as well as grapes and other rich

fruits. The Palmyran god Bel himself was equated with the Greek Zeus and the Roman Jupiter.
Open: 8am–6pm (summer); 8am–4pm (winter). Admission charge.

Valley of Tombs

With over 150 tombs, the Palmyra necropolis is the largest and most impressive in the Middle East after Egypt's Valley of the Kings and Valley of the Queens. The tower tombs date from the 9th century BC to the 2nd century AD and the most spectacular one, the Tomb of Elahbel, can be entered with a ticket and climbed. The other tomb on the ticket is the Tomb of the Three Brothers, located separately in the southwest necropolis, an underground *hypogeum* similar to that of Yarhai in the Damascus National Museum, with fine carvings and paintings inside.
Open: buses run from Palmyra's Archaeological Museum to the site at 8.30am, 10am, 11.30am & 2pm. Admission charge, paid in advance at the museum.

Camels waiting for passengers in the Roman city of Palmyra

The Romans in Syria

In 64 BC the Roman General Pompey invaded, creating the Roman Province of Syria, with Antioch as its metropolis or capital. The province flourished economically and Antioch went on to become the third imperial city after Rome and Alexandria. Damascus, too, was brought under direct Roman rule early in the 1st century AD, and in the 2nd century Bosra was declared the capital of the new Province of Arabia in what is now southern Syria.

A frieze of the Temple of Jupiter, now the Great Umayyad Mosque, in Damascus

QUEEN ZENOBIA

Modelling herself on Cleopatra, from whom she claimed descent, the Palmyrene Queen Zenobia is described to us by early Roman historians as a great beauty with black eyes and pearl-white teeth. She was also a cultured woman, well versed in Greek literature, but she has captured the imagination of later generations primarily for her defiance of Rome and its might. After her husband Regional Governor Odenathus was killed by the Persian Sassanids in 266, and Emperor Gallien died in 267, she declared herself empress of Rome. Sending her armies to occupy Egypt (Rome's granary at the time) and Asia Minor, she conferred onto her son Wahballat, still an infant, all the titles of his father. She thereby set herself up as a direct threat to the new Roman Emperor Aurelian (270–75), who surged into Syria at the head of his armies, defeating her at Antioch and then at Emessa. After a march of 140km (87 miles) across the desert, he captured Palmyra. Zenobia herself fled east but was caught as she tried to cross the Euphrates, possibly in the hope of finding refuge with the Persian king. Some sources say she was killed, while others say she was sent to Rome as a prisoner, later marrying a rich senator.

As Roman control was gradually systematised, networks of roads and forts were built to control the trade in luxury items like silks and precious stones and to defend the frontiers of the empire. Grain and wine also became particular specialities, with

A Roman sarcophagus in the grounds of the National Museum in Damascus

grain grown in the Hauran region to the south of Damascus, and wine in the hinterland of Antioch, where the so-called Cities of the Dead grew up. The main north-south roads were the Via Maris, following the coasts of Syria and Phoenicia, and the Strata Diocletiana from Sura on the Euphrates south through Resafe, Palmyra and Dmeir to Damascus. On average the roads were around 6m (20ft) wide, made of loosely compacted stones.

The Roman forts were mainly concentrated along the eastern frontier to counter the Parthian and later the Sassanid threat. By the end of the 2nd century some six or seven legions were stationed in Syria, thought to be about 30,000–40,000 soldiers, supplemented by locally recruited auxiliaries. Syria's population also made its own contribution, in the form of Julia Domna, daughter of the High Priest of Emessa (Homs), who married Septimius Severus c. AD 187 and went on to become the effective power behind the throne of Caracalla, her son. Later, Syria produced its own Roman emperor, namely Philip the Arab from Shahba, who ruled briefly in the 3rd century.

Walk: Palmyra

This walk should be seen as an introduction to the monuments on the main classical site.

Allowing a little time to look at the buildings themselves, it will take around three hours. With the time and inclination you could extend it another hour or so and walk over into the Valley of Tombs from Diocletian's Camp. The total distance is about 3.5km (2 miles).

Start at the Sanctuary of Bel, the largest building on the site, just off the main road opposite the major grouping of ruins.

1 Sanctuary of Bel

This is the only monument on the walk that has opening times, so make sure your timing conforms (*see pp65–7*).

Cross the road and head for the Monumental Arch at one end of the colonnaded street, about 100m (110yds) to the north.

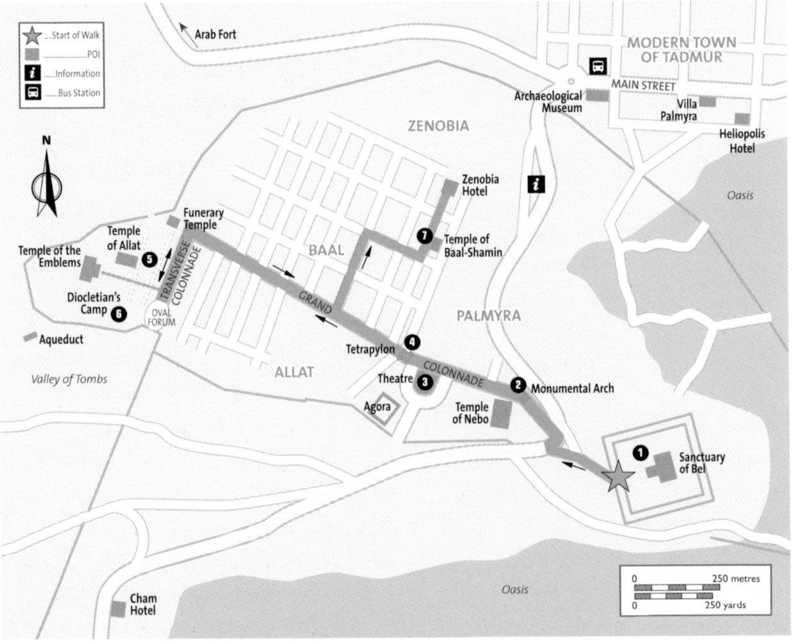

2 Monumental Arch

Built at the peak of Palmyra's prosperity by Septimius Severus (AD 193–211), the double arch has a fan-shaped architecture, ingeniously designed to disguise the 30° change in direction of the colonnaded street. This was necessitated by the pre-existing Temple of Nebo to the left (south) of the street. The Mesopotamian god of oracles, Nebo was identified with Apollo, whose favour was vital, so the street was diverted round his temple.
Walk along the colonnaded street some 200m (220yds) and fork left to the theatre.

3 Theatre

Surprisingly small, this theatre would have been the scene of violent spectacles with wild animals, but is nowadays used for the much gentler performances of singing and dancing in the Palmyra Festival in early May. The decoration of its stage building is especially fine. It was dug out of the sand in 1952.
Behind the theatre have a brief stroll round the agora, senate and tariff court, now heavily ruined, but once the commercial heart of the city. Return to the main street and continue 50m (55yds) to the Tetrapylon.

4 Tetrapylon

This structure of four-pillared podia exists to disguise the 10° change in direction of the colonnaded street. Largely reconstructed in 1963, only one of its pillars is still the original pink Aswan granite, brought from Upper Egypt.
You now have a long stretch of 500m (550yds) along the street to reach a group of temples at the end.

5 Funerary Temple, Temple of Allat and Temple of the Emblems

The temples here have some well-preserved fragments. Allat was a local warrior goddess who protected the nomadic population. The Temple of Emblems has a heavily weathered flight of steps, and at the back you can climb a staircase for fine views over the site.
The area just south of the temples is Diocletian's Camp.

6 Diocletian's Camp

After the fall of Queen Zenobia and the plunder of the city in AD 273, Diocletian garrisoned his soldiers here. Traces have been found of what was thought to be Zenobia's palace, along with an oval piazza similar to that at Jerash in Jordan.
Retrace your steps along the Colonnade and head north for about 200m (220yds) to reach the Temple of Baal-Shamin.

7 Temple of Baal-Shamin

The best-preserved building after the Sanctuary of Bel, this little gem dates from AD 150 and is dedicated to the Canaanite deity of rain and fertility. In Byzantine times it served as a church.
Reward yourself now with a drink on the terrace of the Zenobia Hotel, just 75m (80yds) away, overlooking the ruins.

Sites of the desert and Euphrates Valley

Only those with more than a week to spend in Syria, or those perhaps on a second trip to the country, venture east from Palmyra. The distances are big, with Deir Ez-Zour, the main town on the Euphrates, a full 201km (125 miles) northeast from Palmyra, through featureless, inhospitable steppe-land, but the rewards are worthwhile, in the form of unusual sites, unlike any found elsewhere in Syria.

At least one overnight stay is required here, to visit the two sites of Doura Europos, 93km (58 miles) to the south, and Mari, 31km (19 miles) further south still, then to follow the Euphrates Valley northwest to Aleppo. Driving your own car is faster and more convenient than any public transport options, and roads are good and clearly signposted for all the listings below.

Doura Europos

One hour's drive south from Deir Ez-Zour, the ruins of this immense Hellenistic fortress city form the most impressive site in the Euphrates Valley. Their setting is at first difficult to appreciate, as the approach is from behind, with no sign of the river, but once you have entered the site through the massive 9m (30ft) high ramparts, you begin to see, as you head over towards the edge of the cliff, what a commanding location it enjoys.

Known primarily for the ancient synagogue which was taken piece by piece in the 1930s and reassembled in the Damascus National Museum, the site today is remarkable not only for its setting, but also for the combination of buildings it gathers together. Located as it was on the edge of the Roman and Parthian empires, it boasts 16 temples in which Jews, Christians and pagans all worshipped together. Over to the far left of the entrance is the area of the 3rd-century Roman military camp, complete with commander's palace. Down at the edge of the river on its own outcrop guarding the bend in the river is the fine Seleucid citadel. The site is extensive and you should allow a good hour or more for a visit.

Note that there are no facilities. *Open: 9am–6pm (summer); 9am–4pm (winter). Admission charge.*

Halabiye

After Doura Europos the site of Halabiye is the most striking in the Euphrates Valley. Located 56km (35 miles) northwest of Deir Ez-Zour, it is on the road to Aleppo, which is 246km (153 miles) further to the northwest. Clinging to a steep hillside directly above the river, it consists of a dramatic Byzantine fortification dating from the 6th century when Emperor Justinian was fortifying it as a northern outpost against the Persian threat. Most impressive of all are the three-storey imperial barracks built into the side of the defensive wall near the summit of the fort.

There are no facilities on site.
Open unfenced site. Admission charge.

Mari

Tucked right down in the extreme southeast corner of the country near the Iraqi border, 31km (19 miles) beyond Doura Europos, the site of Mari is of unique importance archaeologically. Not only is it a rare example of a Bronze Age Mesopotamian palace, but also its 15,000 clay archives in Akkadian (old Babylonian, an ancient Semitic language) were found intact, providing an exceptional source of information on the early history of the region.

Doura Europos, with the Euphrates River running by

Excavations were ongoing here from 1933 (when it was first discovered by accident) until 1974 by the eminent French archaeologist Andre Parrot. Post-1978 excavations have continued, still by the French. Many of the best early finds are in the Louvre in Paris, which funded the early excavations.

As a royal city-state of the 3rd millennium BC, Mari controlled the caravan routes from central and southern Mesopotamia up to the confluence of the Khabour and Euphrates rivers to the north. It boasted a sophisticated irrigation system, with a canal that made a loop inward from the Euphrates, where boats could moor safely away from the river currents.

Inside Zimri-Lim palace at Mari

The palace itself is the most extensively excavated part of the site, difficult for the non-specialist to appreciate, originally with around 300 rooms, named after Mari's last ruler Zimri-Lim (1775–1760 BC). It was sacked and burnt by Hammurabi of Babylon in 1760 BC and never used again.

The site has little shade except when inside the roofed palace, so come prepared. A visit takes about an hour as the site covers quite a large area. There's a simple café and facilities.

Open: 8am–dusk. Admission charge.

Qal'at Ar-Rahba

On the way to Doura Europos, some 40km (25 miles) south of Deir Ez-Zour, the almost fairy-tale castle of Qal'at Ar-Rahba rises up to the right of the main road as if in a mirage. Dating to the 12th century, the castle was built by Nur Ed-Din, unifier of Syria against the Crusaders, then destroyed a century later by the Mongol invasion and abandoned.

No facilities.

Open unfenced site. Free admission.

Qasr Al-Hayr Ash-Sharqi

Located 120km (75 miles) northeast of Palmyra and 160km (100 miles) southwest of Deir Ez-Zour, this is Syria's one proper example of an Umayyad desert palace, a refuge of the caliphs from city life and the tedious business of administering their newly conquered empire. Most of these palaces lie further south in what is now

Jordan or the West Bank. A tarmac road leads to it so it can be reached by saloon car. The interesting decoration is concentrated on the monumental gateway, a mix of Byzantine, Persian and Mesopotamian styles.

No facilities.

Open unfenced site. Admission charge.

Resafe

Located all by itself in the middle of nowhere, 197km (122 miles) southeast of Aleppo and 194km (120 miles) northwest of Deir Ez-Zour, the remarkable site of Resafe is Syria's most dramatic and impressive Byzantine city. The circumference of the walls is over 2km (1¼ miles) and they loom up out of the desert as you approach, enclosing a vast enclosure measuring 550m by 400m (600yds by 440yds). The original town here was built by the Romans in the 3rd century, but grew larger with the cult of St Sergius here in Byzantine times, a Roman soldier who was martyred for refusing to make a sacrifice to Jupiter. The St Sergius basilica on the site is today the most impressive, dated to 559, a large triple-aisled building with very fine stonework. The nave has a large *bema*, a raised area where the clergy would have sat. Look out, too, for the three enormous underground cisterns where the town's water was stored.

Simple café facilities are on site.

Open unfenced site. Free admission.

The main gate of Qasr Al-Hayr Ash-Sharqi

The Orontes Valley and Cities of the Dead

This region of Syria is possibly the most surprising and unexpected. There is no hint of desert, the rich soil of the Orontes Valley boasting great fertility. Most of Syria's agricultural produce is grown here, and the powerful Roman city of Apamea was positioned to dominate the valley. Homs and Hama, the third- and fourth-largest cities of Syria respectively, are both located on the banks of the Orontes, with Hama famous for its magnificent old waterwheels, devised to lift the water from the river to irrigate the higher ground via aqueducts.

Two huge Bronze Age sites can also be visited in this area, both contemporary with Mari in the Euphrates Valley, and, as with Mari, excavations are still ongoing and bringing to light further finds each season which are helping to piece together the ancient history of this highly advanced region.

Also totally unexpected are the extraordinary relics to be found in the limestone foothills of the mountains north of Apamea and to the north and west of Aleppo. Scattered about on the hillsides here, often in dramatic locations on ridges and summits, are the so-called Cities of the Dead or Dead Cities. No less than 700 have been identified so far and, again, digs are ongoing each season, revealing new evidence and uncovering the secrets of these fascinating sites. Dating from the 1st to the 6th centuries, they include over 2,000 monasteries and churches from the early days of Christianity in this country. About a dozen or so of these Cities of the Dead are in such a good state of preservation, built as they were of the local limestone, that they resemble ghost towns,

The relic of the Virgin's Belt in Homs (*see p83*)

abandoned almost overnight, which is how they acquired their exotic name. An application is under way for the whole area to be declared a UNESCO World Heritage Site, Syria's sixth, after the Old Cities of Damascus and Aleppo, Bosra theatre, Palmyra and Krak des Chevaliers.

Their wealth was built on the cultivation of vines for wine and olives for olive oil, as can be seen from the presses found in their centres, but when this trade stopped, the population dwindled and moved elsewhere. The region only started to become repopulated towards the end of the 19th century.

Tourist-level accommodation is limited in the area, and most visitors explore the Cities of the Dead from a base of either Hama or Aleppo. Any visit to Syria should include if at all possible a day or two devoted to the exploration of these remarkable sites. Space permits only the major ones to be covered here.

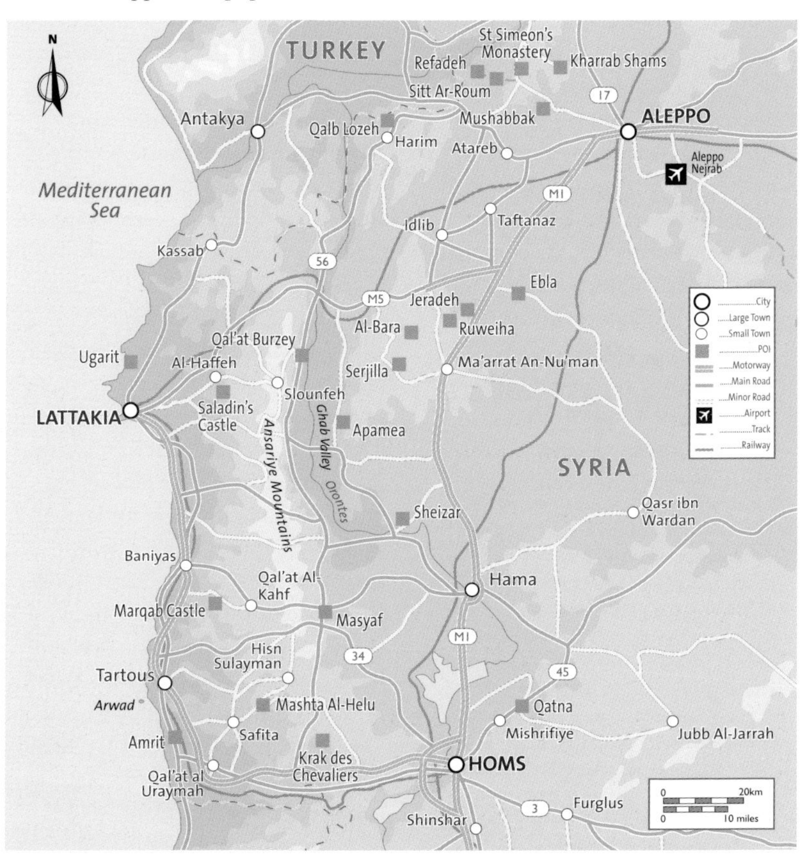

APAMEA AND SHEIZAR

Apamea

Most people visiting Syria for the first time will never have heard of Apamea, yet it is in fact the country's largest classical site, covering 200 hectares (494 acres) compared to Palmyra's 50 hectares (124 acres). Its rampart walls still stand 10m (33ft) high in places and were originally 16km (10 miles) long with over 100 towers. As in Palmyra, the necropolis lies outside the walls. The site is 55km (34 miles) northwest of Hama, via Sheizar. If you do not have a car, you need to get a taxi from Hama as public transport is very limited.

Known as Afaamia in Arabic, Apamea is sometimes also signposted 'Qal'at Al-Mudiq', the name of the 12th-century castle that sits on a citadel mound above the site, which was occupied by Crusader knights before the Zengid ruler Nur Ed-Din wrested it from them.

The site itself was first inhabited in the early Bronze Age, but at its peak in the 3rd century BC its population was estimated by ancient historians to be 500,000 (some 380,000 of whom were slaves), with 40,000 horses and 500 fighting elephants, the rich pastureland well able to support such numbers. The nearby Orontes was used for irrigation and there were also three lakes close at hand.

Belgian excavators began digs here in 1930, continuing for over 50 years, but work is far from over. Many of the best early finds were transported to a museum in Brussels, which was then bombed in World War II, destroying almost everything. The remaining items, especially mosaics, are on view in the site museum set in the Ottoman caravanserai near the entrance.

Without doubt the most evocative aspect of the site is its Grand Colonnade of over 1,200 columns, 400 of which have been re-erected in recent decades. This makes it one of the longest and most beautiful avenues of the ancient world, over 2km (1¼ miles) long, compared to Palmyra's 1.2km (¾ mile). Over the centuries many columns had fallen from war and earthquakes, and those especially associated with Apamea are the distinctive spiral-fluted ones. The theatre here, now heavily ruined and pillaged as a local quarry, was the largest in Syria with a 139m (456ft) diameter, compared with Bosra's

AN ARAB-SYRIAN GENTLEMAN

At the age of 90, the warrior-prince Usama Bin Munqidh, lord of Sheizar Castle, wrote his memoirs, giving us one of the very few accounts we have from an Arab viewpoint of the Frankish Crusaders as they entered Syria en route to Jerusalem. A contemporary of Saladin, he died in 1188, one year after the Battle of Hittin where the Crusaders were famously beaten. Wittily written and containing many earthy observations about the strange customs of the Franks, the book was translated into English by Philip K Hitti in 1987 under the title *An Arab-Syrian Gentleman and Warrior in the Period of the Crusades*, and is highly recommended.

90m (295ft), and dates from the 2nd century.

Simple café facilities on site.

Open unfenced site. Admission charge.

Sheizar

Just 28km (17½ miles) from Hama, a brief stop here on the way to Apamea will be rewarded with a fine view down into the Orontes gorge behind the 12th-century fortification that stands here on a rocky outcrop above the town. Just outside the town, notice the 11-arched Roman bridge to the right of the road.

Open site. Free admission.

The approach to Apamea

EBLA AND HAMA

Ebla

Clearly signposted as Tell Mardikh and lying to the east of the Damascus-Aleppo highway, Ebla is Syria's most important Bronze Age site, lying 60km (37 miles) south of Aleppo. As with all sites dating from the 3rd and 2nd millennium BC, you need to use your imagination to conjure up what it would once have looked like, though the sheer scale remains impressive. It covers a vast area of 56 hectares (138 acres), with the acropolis in the centre, where most of the excavations have been concentrated. The north-south axis of the city was approximately 1km (2/3 mile) while the east-west axis was 0.7km (½ mile). The defensive earthwork ramparts were up to 40m (131ft) thick at their base and up to 22m (72ft) high.

The excavations here have been the life's work of Professor Paolo Matthiae, whose Italian archaeological expedition discovered the site in 1964. The name of Ebla was known to be a major trading and political centre, through archives found earlier at Mari and even in Hittite texts and on the walls of Karnak in ancient Egypt. But it was not until a statue of a king of Ebla was found in 1968, dating to 2000 BC, that the city's identity was suspected, later to be confirmed absolutely by the discovery of over 17,000 clay tablets in the archive of the royal palace. This palace occupies most of the acropolis, and, apart from the residential quarters, included kitchens, stores and workshops. The bulk of the finds are on display at Idlib museum, 20km (12 miles) away.

There are simple facilities on site.
Open site. Admission charge.

WATERWHEELS

Known as *norias* in Arabic, the earliest ones are known to have existed as long ago as the 5th century, from a mosaic dated AD 469. Around 100 existed at one time, but now only 17 remain, ranging in diameter from 7m to 21m (23ft to 69ft). Driven by the current of the river, the earliest of those remaining date from the 14th and 15th centuries, and the largest one has 120 wooden scooping bowls to lift the water up to the aqueducts that used to carry it off to the higher-level fields for irrigation.

Hama

Hama is situated 146km (91 miles) south of Aleppo and 209km (130 miles) north of Damascus, so it is the obvious overnight base between the two main centres. However, Hama also deserves a visit in its own right, for it has probably Syria's most charming town centre, arranged along the banks of the Orontes River, dotted with spectacularly large ancient wooden waterwheels. Still in use, they moan and creak with their unmistakeable sound, known as their 'voice', from which experts can diagnose their exact state of health.

Apart from a stroll along the riverbank, the town offers two other main attractions.

Azem Palace

A perfect little gem of a palace, this 18th-century building stands right on the river, and served as a private residence until 1920. All on a small scale, the courtyards are exquisitely decorated with beautiful floors of coloured marble, basalt and porphyry.

Open: 9am–2pm. Closed: Tue. Admission charge.

Hama Museum

The fine mosaics here include the Mosaic of the Noria and the Female Musicians, dated to the late 4th century.

Open: 9am–2pm. Closed: Tue. Admission charge.

One of the waterwheels in Hama

HOMS AND QATNA

Homs

Almost equidistant between Damascus and Aleppo on the main north-south highway, Homs lies 47km (29 miles) south of Hama. Syria's third city after Damascus and Aleppo, Homs today buzzes with activity. It is the country's industrial heartland, with oil refineries, sugar refineries and the bulk of the country's factories. This makes certain parts of it visually unprepossessing, but

The citadel at Homs

do not be too easily put off, for Homs has a few surprising charms, and the countryside around it, especially to the east as you approach from the Palmyra side, is remarkably green and fertile, with extensive orchards of fruit and almond trees.

Its position here was chosen for strategic reasons, controlling what is known as the Homs Gap, the break in the mountains between the coastal plain and the desert. Today it also sits on the natural crossroads of Syria's road and rail networks.

As ancient Emessa it dates back to the 2nd century BC, and its citadel mound from that period can still be seen on the edge of town. Currently under excavation by a British team, there have been some interesting finds, but little remains for the layman beyond the Hellenistic foundation stones.

In the centre of town you can stroll in the old covered souks and also visit the adjacent Great Mosque, which lies on the site of the Church of St John. The large, imposing Ottoman mosque set beside a park is named after Khalid Ibn Al-Walid, conqueror of Syria, whose tomb reputedly lies inside.

Homs' more surprising secrets are its two early churches, to be found in the Christian Quarter west of the Great Mosque and the souks. The curiously named Church of the Virgin's Belt boasts in its side chapel, under the altar, the belt supposedly taken from the Virgin Mary's robe.

JULIA DOMNA

Homs was celebrated as the birthplace of Julia Domna, daughter of the High Priest of Emessa. A formidable lady, well read in philosophy, her hand in marriage was requested by the Roman Emperor Septimius Severus *c.* AD 187 because of her horoscope predicting her as queen. The marriage was a happy one and, unusually, she accompanied her husband on his campaigns, even visiting Britain with him. She gave him two sons, Geta and Caracalla, both of whom went on to become emperor in their turn, with her as the power behind the throne. Coins were even minted with her portrait.

Some 300m (330yds) further on is the more interesting Church of St Elian, whose frescoes, discovered in 1970 under more modern ones, date back to the 6th century, making them possibly the oldest in Syria. Both churches are in use and always open and a guardian will gladly show you round. There is no admission charge but a donation to the church's box will be welcome. Leave some coins if you light a candle.

Qatna

Rarely visited but just 15km (9 miles) to the northeast of Homs is the Bronze Age city of Qatna, whose impressive ramparts can still be seen, along with the foundations of a temple and palace, dating to the 14th century BC. The modern village nearby is called Mishrifiye, whose inhabitants had to be moved out of the ancient site so that excavations could begin.

Open unfenced site. Free admission.

SOUTHERN CITIES OF THE DEAD

The sites below constitute the major, most easily visitable of the southern Dead Cities. All are unfenced sites and have free admission. There are no facilities at any of them. Details on how to reach them all are provided in the driving route (*see pp86–7*).

Al-Bara

This is the largest of any of the Dead Cities, with an estimated population of 5,000 once boasting five churches, three monasteries and many fine villas. A tarmac road links the various parts of the ruins, sparing you the fatigue of clambering around in the undergrowth across the hillsides and valleys.

It is best to start at Deir Sobat, a beautiful two-storey building standing by itself in a bucolic setting overlooking olive groves, and thought either to have been a monastery of the 6th century or a rich villa with balconies and a garden. It is the first main building you arrive at after following the tarmac road, about 2km (1¼ miles) beyond the village of Al-Bara.

Some 300m (330yds) further on is a massive pyramid tomb containing five heavily carved sarcophagi, conveying the wealth of their owners. Across the field opposite the tomb you can walk over to inspect the communal wine press, and then, in the field after that, the town's olive press, semi-underground with a massive grinding stone which a pair of donkeys would have pulled round and round. The other major buildings are a church known as Al-Husn, meaning 'the fort', and a second pyramid tomb.

Jeradeh

Surrounded by pistachio trees and set on the edge of the mountain range, Jeradeh's finest building is its six-storey hermit tower, complete with latrine-like machicolation boxes on the top (from where missiles were thrown down onto attackers). It also has an elegant porticoed villa fronting onto a courtyard which now serves as the village football pitch.

Ruweiha

These attractive ruins have been charmingly incorporated into the local villagers' lives, with the fine early Church of Bissos, one of the largest in the country, doubling as a giant animal pen. The villagers do not mind visitors, however, and will frequently offer tea. The setting is pretty, with views over the foothills.

Serjilla

This is probably the closest there is among the Dead Cities to the most perfectly preserved little town, still with a sense of completeness. Its remote setting in a barren landscape emphasises this, as there is no nearby settlement and it is thus totally silent. Even the road on which it stands is a dead end.

The path leads down into the centre, passing a group of scattered sarcophagi, the dead being buried beyond the perimeter of the town as was the norm, and leads on into a little open square, most unusual in the Cities of the Dead, this being one of the rare examples. Just off the square is the public baths building, well preserved and complete with caldarium and frigidarium, and very interesting in terms of being Christian rather than Roman baths. They are dated to 473 by a mosaic originally found on the floor by an American expedition in 1899, but this has since vanished. The other building off the square is the men's meeting room, known as an *andron*, the only one of its kind among the Dead Cities. Its double-porticoed façade is very fine and hints at the wealth once enjoyed here. Nearby are a church dated to 372 and a group of two-storey villas again suggestive of great wealth. Some of the houses have their own olive presses.

A two-storey villa in Serjilla

Drive: Cities of the Dead

Starting from Hama, the best place to stay in the area, this tour takes you along dual carriageways and small tarmac country roads. It offers the chance to experience the natural beauty of Syria's more remote countryside.

This is a full day trip, and you should take food and water as there are very limited eating places in the area. The total distance is about 160km (100 miles).

Set out from Hama on the main highway north towards Aleppo till you reach Ma'arrat An-Nu'man after about 50km (31 miles). Fork west towards Kafr Nabel, 10km (6 miles) away. In the centre of Kafr Nabel turn right at the crossroads for Serjilla and Al-Bara, and after 8km (5 miles) turn right for Serjilla, which is 3.5km (2¼ miles) further on.

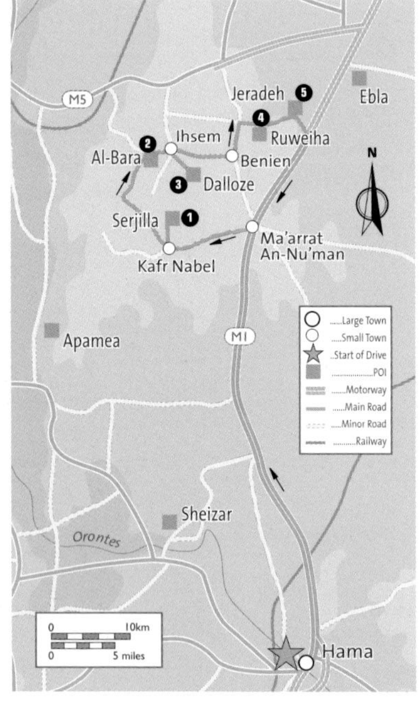

1 Serjilla

Sitting by itself at the end of the road is what can rightly be considered one of Syria's most haunting sights. Nestled in a hollow in a wild and desolate landscape is the abandoned ghost town of Serjilla (*see pp84–5*).

Allow one hour.

Open site. Free admission.

Return to the junction and take the fork for Al-Bara which you come to almost immediately. From the centre of the modern town, take the road to the left at the corner of the school, which leads down to the ancient site, forking left at the first junction.

2 Al-Bara

As a very extensive site covering an area 3km by 2km (1¾ miles by 1¼ miles), an exploration of Al-Bara involves a lot of walking and takes about two hours (*see p84*).

Return to the centre of Al-Bara, and continue north to Ihsem. At the entrance to the village take the road right, continuing for 3.6km (2¼ miles) to reach Dalloze.

3 Dalloze

In this tiny hamlet is a cluster of ancient stone houses in a remarkable state of preservation, their courtyards, doors and windows beautifully crafted.

Return to Ihsem and in the village turn right. After Benien follow the new road to Idlib, and 4km (2½ miles) later Ruweiha is signed as 5km (3 miles) from crossroads.

4 Ruweiha

Twenty-five kilometres (15½ miles) on from Al-Bara this extensive Dead City is located beside a modern village and has a very fine church (*see p84*).

Continue just 2km (1¼ miles) further to reach Jeradeh.

5 Jeradeh

Remarkable for its six-storey hermit's tower, the ruins of Jeradeh have a pretty setting on the edge of a village overlooking the plains to the west (*see p84*).

From here you continue east to rejoin the main Damascus highway to the south, returning to Hama.

A view over Al-Bara, the largest of the Dead Cities

Byzantine Syria

By the time Emperor Constantine officially recognised Christianity as the state religion in 313, Syria was already heavily Christian, thanks to the early missions of St Paul and other disciples. Constantine's mother, Helen, started a trend for pilgrimages to Jerusalem and other holy sites in Syria, and when Byzantium (later renamed Constantinople, now Istanbul) split from Rome and was adopted as the second capital in 395, the divide between the eastern and western strands of the church set the scene for the Byzantine era (395–636).

In spite of the deep divisions that racked the church throughout the 4th, 5th and 6th centuries, in Syria it was a time of prosperity, based on

The baths and meeting room at the Byzantine town of Serjilla

A Byzantine tomb door made of black basalt, bearing the cross of Byzantium

agricultural export of olive oil, wine and wheat. This prosperity was reflected in a flurry of building projects, and by the 5th and 6th centuries, Syria was dotted with numerous churches and many monasteries, another surprising facet of what Syria has to offer now. Indeed, nowhere else in the Mediterranean world will you find such a concentration of Byzantine churches, villages and monasteries.

Throughout the 6th and early 7th centuries, Syria's frontiers to the east were under increasing threat from the Persian Sassanids, the period from which the fortifications at Resafe and Halabiye date. Emperor Justinian (527–65) fought many wars against them on Syrian soil, and a series of earthquakes also ravaged the population. Weakened by centuries of warfare between the Roman and Persian worlds, Byzantine Syria was exhausted, and lay as easy pickings for the new force that entered from the south in 636: the armies of Islam.

CITIES OF THE DEAD

First rediscovered in 1860 by a French aristocrat, scholars have now identified 780 of these Byzantine ghost towns, with over 2,000 churches, spread over an area of 140km by 30km (87 miles by 19 miles) in the foothills of the mountains north of Hama and west of Aleppo. Of these, around 100 are sizeable, with around 30 forming the core of those most visited. It would take at least a month to see them all properly, and most visitors spend a day or two at best. Most are at altitudes of 400–500m (1,310–1,640ft), and a few are on outcrops as high as 800m (2,625ft).

Abandoned in the hills for over ten centuries, they have come down to us remarkably unscathed, thanks to the fact that they were built from the local white limestone, wood being in short supply. No cement was used to bind the stones, but the building techniques were simple and solid. The communities living here were based on the export of wine and olive oil to the Mediterranean via the port of Antioch. Wine and olive presses are found in abundance throughout the settlements, and the price of olive oil is known to have boomed in the 5th century. However, nothing lasts forever, and when the trade routes were disrupted by wars between Byzantines and invading Arabs, the livelihood of the villagers was destroyed and they were forced to leave the hills and move closer to the coast to find new ways of making a living.

ST SIMEON'S MONASTERY

Of all Syria's Byzantine remains, pride of place must go the basilica and monastic complex of St Simeon, built on top of its own mound in the hills 42km (26 miles) northwest of Aleppo, from whose centre it is well signposted. Some scholars have even claimed that the magnificence of the stone craftsmanship in the details such as arches, friezes, cornices and door lintels is the forerunner of the sculptured ornamentation of Byzantium. The complex can be visited as an easy half-day taxi or car excursion from Aleppo, or incorporated into a full day's circuit of other sites around Aleppo, such as Kharrab Shams, Mushabbak and Sitt Ar-Roum (*see pp92–3*).

A massively important pilgrimage centre, all roads in northern Syria led to this great church and monastery erected at the foot of Saint Simeon's pillar.

The site has the feel of a sacred, holy place, thanks to its wooded setting. Though it can get very busy with hundreds of visitors a day, if you are here early or, better still, late, the silence and the wind in the trees can be very evocative.

Look out on the wall of the ticket office for the picture showing a

The remains of the saint's column (now topped with a boulder)

ST SIMEON OF THE PILLAR

The son of a local farmer, Simeon had a monastic calling from an early age, moving to a cave on the hill where the basilica now stands and leading a life of severe austerity. He wore spikes that drew blood, chained himself to a rock and buried himself up to the chin in full summer. As news of this strange behaviour spread, people began to seek him out to see for themselves, much to Simeon's annoyance. To escape their attentions, he took to living on top of a pillar, first 3m (10ft) high, then 6m (20ft), then 11m (36ft) and finally 18m (59ft), the height increasing for greater privacy as the crowds grew, seeking miracles from him. He was brought food once a week by his disciples and a railing was built round his pillar to stop him falling off in his sleep. The Greek for pillar, stylos, has given us his name, Simeon Stylites. The visitors to his pillar became increasingly important, and he began to preach twice a day, warning against the dangers of earthly vices and describing the rewards of heaven that awaited the pious. He died in 459 after spending 36 years on top of his pillar, and the emperor sent 600 soldiers to carry his body to Constantinople. His feast day is 5 January in the West, 27 July among the Syrian Orthodox and 1 September in the Eastern Orthodox Church.

reconstruction of the complex, complete with dome at the centre of four basilicas making the shape of the cross. Seen in the context of the religious politics of the time, the massive construction was an imperial statement announcing the supremacy of Byzantine orthodoxy in the region over the heretic rival Monophysites based in Antioch. Hence the emperor Zenon sent skilled architects and artisans to carry out the project to the highest standards.

The original approach was from the Via Sacra, the Pilgrims' Path, still marked by a fine gateway on the opposite side of the hill, which snaked its way up from Deir Semaan (ancient Telanissos), the village that grew up in the valley below to house the pilgrims. The remains of ancient stone-built inns and hostelries can still be seen scattered among today's modern village houses.

A short path leads up from the ticket office to the flat summit, from where the church/monastery complex is to your right, and the baptistery 200m (220yds) off to your left. The triple-arched façade of the church is stunning in its delicacy, and the whole complex took 14 years to build. On completion in 490 it was the largest and most important church in the world, later surpassed only by Ayia Sofia in Constantinople, and not equalled in Europe till the 11th and 12th centuries.

There are simple café facilities on site.

Open: 9am–6pm (summer); 9am–4pm (winter). Admission charge.

The impressive triple-arched façade of St Simeon's Monastery

CITIES OF THE DEAD WEST OF ALEPPO

This cluster of Dead Cities lies in the hills west of Aleppo and all can be visited together in a long day trip from a base of Aleppo, though Qalb Lozeh might be better incorporated into a trip from Aleppo to Lattakia on the coast. All are open, unfenced sites, except Qalb Lozeh, which requires an entry fee. None has any facilities, so go prepared with your own refreshments.

Kharrab Shams

One of the most rural and photogenic of all the Dead Cities, charmingly situated far from any nearby settlement, Kharrab Shams lies 12km (7½ miles) east of St Simeon. The church is especially elegant, its side aisles having collapsed long ago, revealing the central nave to be almost perfectly preserved, with five graceful arches surmounted by ten windows. Dated to 372, it is one of the oldest churches in the area. An oak tree grows in the middle of the altar.

During the Arab period the church was turned into a little fort and a wall built across the nave, conserving by happy chance the carved chancel rail behind it, the only one of its kind to survive in the whole country. Further up the hillside are clusters of ruined houses and another later church, possibly part of a monastery complex.

Mushabbak

On the road out to St Simeon, 25km (15½ miles) west of Aleppo, you will see the fine 5th-century church up on the ridge to the left, reached by a track off the main road. It was probably used as a staging post by pilgrims en route to St Simeon. Very well preserved, it still has its nave and both aisles to the full height, with nine arched windows on the upper level. On the north side, steps cut into the rock lead down to a subterranean tomb.

Qalb Lozeh

This remarkable church, 42km (26 miles) southwest of St Simeon, stands at an altitude of 683m (2,240ft) in the hills west of Aleppo. It is reached by forking left off the road to Harim and climbing 13km (8 miles) up into the hills, through the Druze village of Bnabel. Just before Qalb Lozeh are the remains of a cluster of houses, churches and a hermit's tower, known as Kirkbezeh.

Widely seen as one of Syria's best examples of what we in Europe would recognise as Romanesque architecture, the church of Qalb Lozeh boasts a flamboyant entrance façade flanked by twin square towers, the first known example of such a style anywhere in the world.

Open: 9am–4pm. Admission charge.

Sitt Ar-Roum and Refadeh

Situated just before St Simeon, these two sites are reached by branching off left to Qatoura, 3km (1¾ miles) off the main road. Sitt Ar-Roum lies barely 1km (²/₃ mile) beyond the village, where a well-preserved 5th-century church nave still stands. Continuing along the same track for another 1km (2/3 mile), you will come to the ruins of Refadeh, signalled by a 9m (30ft) tall watchtower. Set a little way off from the modern village, the spot is usually deserted. There is no church here, but behind the tower are some impressive private houses, the grandest of which has a double colonnaded loggia with a tower at either end.

The 5th-century church at Mushabbak

Aleppo and the north

Aleppo is the obvious base for any tour of northern Syria, very different in feel to southern Syria. Aleppo itself, too, is very different from Damascus, the city with which it has traditionally vied for two titles: oldest continuously inhabited city in the world, and commercial capital of Syria. Much of Aleppo's flair for commerce comes from the dynamic Christian community which has long thrived here, encouraging trade with Europe and the West.

The wider avenues and green open spaces of modern Aleppo are thanks to the French Mandate, when much of the city was re-planned, but the old heart of the city remains much as it ever was; the souks in particular, vestiges of the Middle Ages, have remained unchanged for centuries.

History

Settled for over eight millennia, the earliest records of the city, known as

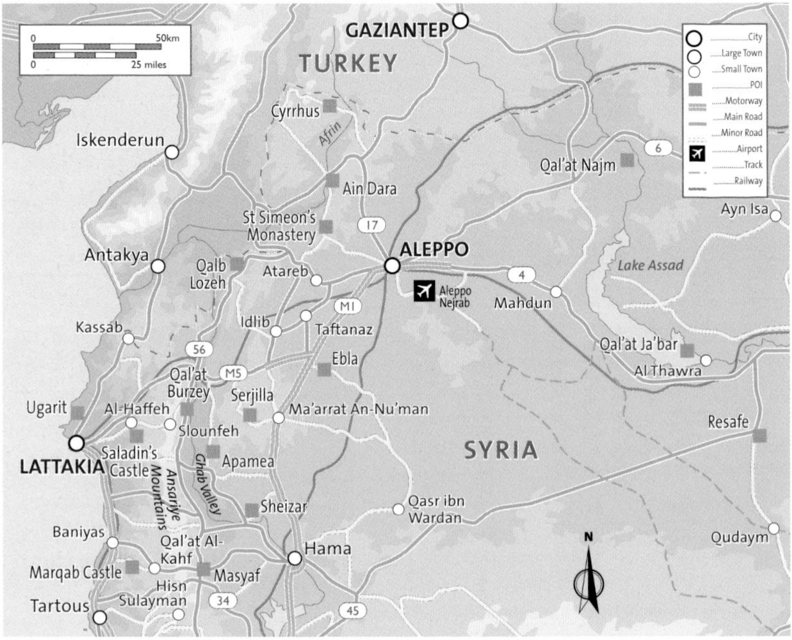

Halap (from which today's Arabic name of Halab comes), appear in the archives of Mari and of the Hittites. Unlike Damascus, whose links were mainly to the south, Aleppo's connections were largely north towards Turkey and east to Mesopotamia. It was at one stage capital of a neo-Hittite state.

After Alexander the Great's conquest, his general, Seleucus Nicator, founded the town of Beroia at the foot of the mound on which the ancient town (now the citadel) was built. As with all such Hellenistic cities, it was laid out on a grid system within walls, most of which have long since disappeared. Throughout the 1st millennium Aleppo enjoyed a close rapport with Rome first, then Constantinople, and Christians fleeing from persecution flocked to the remote limestone hills, building what are now known as the Dead Cities.

In 637, Aleppo surrendered to the Muslim armies who surged up from the south, and the city went on to become a powerful centre as capital of the Hamdanid dynasty (944–1003). Emir Sayf Ad-Dawla established a flourishing court, giving patronage to the leading Arab poets of the time, Al-Mutannabi and Abu Firas.

In the next few centuries it was caught up in fighting first with the Byzantine armies, then the Seljuk Turks, then against the invading Crusaders. In 1170 a massive earthquake destroyed much of the city, necessitating extensive rebuilding, and

Houses in Aleppo's Old City

under the Ayyubids (1176–1260) the citadel was restored and many mosques and madrasas were built to reassert Sunni orthodoxy. From the 13th to the 16th centuries the Mamelukes ruled the area, and Aleppo became the trade centre for silks, spices and precious metals from the East headed for the Mediterranean, with huge warehouses (*khans*) to store the goods.

When the Ottomans pushed the Mamelukes out in 1516, Aleppo became the main entrepôt of the Levant, with favoured status given to Venetian, French, English and Dutch merchants. Christian and Jewish communities were given protected status, and after World War I large numbers of Armenian refugees also settled in the city. Trade was badly hit, however, in the 20th century when Hatay Province was awarded to Turkey by the Allies in 1939, thereby cutting Aleppo off from its natural seaport, Antioch (Antakya).

ALEPPO OLD CITY

Al-Jdaideh Christian Quarter

After the old souks, this is Aleppo's most charming and attractive area (*see map, p98*), which grew up in the late Mameluke period (hence its name 'New Quarter') as Maronite and Armenian Christians came to settle here about 1km ($^2/_3$ mile) north of the citadel, drawn by the Venetian trading prosperity. The quarter, with its flagstone streets and elegant residences, even has a Venetian flavour to it, blended with local Arab styles. Several houses have been converted to boutique hotels or restaurants, and one has been converted to the Museum of Popular Arts and Traditions, a beautiful 18th-century courtyard house, restored and furnished to show how life was lived.

Open: 8am–2pm. Closed: Tue. Admission charge.

Archaeological Museum

Located about 1km ($^2/_3$ mile) northwest of the citadel (*see map, p98*), you should allow a good hour to look round this small museum, spread over two floors. The most impressive exhibits are in Room 1, with statues and objects from Mari, Tell Halaf and Ugarit, notably the lion statue, the goddess statue with the pouring vase, and a pair of gold cups. Room 2 also has some remarkable Phoenician ivory plaques.

Open: 9am–6pm. Closed: Tue. Admission charge.

Bimaristan Arghoun

This extraordinary place tucked down a side street in the Old City (*see map, p98*) is the best-preserved Muslim hospital in Syria, and was still in use till the early 20th century. Dating to the 14th century, with three courtyards, it was an institution for the treatment of mental patients using the calming influences of music, water and nature, together with a simple vegetarian diet and herbal teas. It had a policy of complete rehabilitation in the community and no repeat admissions, at a time when in the West mental sufferers were abused and imprisoned.

Open: 9am–6pm (summer); 9am–4pm (winter). Closed: Tue (all year). Admission charge.

Faradis Madrasa

This 13th-century Koranic school, whose name means 'School of Paradise', lies 1km ($^2/_3$ mile) south of the citadel (*see map, p98*) in a scruffy suburb, but is worth visiting for its architecture, considered one of the most elegant buildings of Aleppo. It is still a working institution, and the guardian provides gowns to enable women to enter the prayer hall.

Open: daylight hours. Free admission.

Great Mosque

Notable more for its fine 11th-century Seljuk minaret than for its prayer hall, Aleppo's Great Mosque was founded ten years after the Damascus Great

Mosque but does not compare in terms of grandeur and atmosphere. Much of its earlier fine stonework, which had been taken from the cathedral of Cyrrhus in the north, was stripped by the Abbasids and taken to Baghdad. The only structure of any age left inside is therefore the 14th-century *minbar* (stepped pulpit) with fine ivory and mother-of-pearl inlay.
In the heart of the souks and Old City (see map, p98)*. Open to visitors except during prayer times.*
Free admission.

Madrasa Halawiye

Just opposite the Great Mosque, this building was once the 6th-century Cathedral of St Helena, mother of Constantine, the first emperor to adopt Christianity. Inside the prayer hall you can still see the six huge pink marble columns complete with Corinthian capitals, relics of the cathedral. Christians continued to use the cathedral freely till 1124, a privilege which was only withdrawn that year in retaliation for Crusader atrocities.
Open: daylight hours. Free admission.

An old street in Aleppo's Christian Quarter

Walk: Old Aleppo

This walk is best done in the morning because of opening times. The souks are open from 10am until 10pm. The ground is all on the flat, though uneven underfoot in many of the souk areas, so flat footwear is recommended.

Done at a leisurely pace, and visiting the monuments, the walk will take up to half a day. The total distance is about 2km (1¼ miles).

From the foot of the citadel entrance ramp but on the opposite side of the road, begin by walking 100m (110yds) past the Sultaniye Madrasa and the Governorate building to reach the Hammam Yalbougha.

1 Hammam Yalbougha

These are the grandest baths in Syria, now restored, with a magnificent 14th-century exterior (*see p100*).

Retrace your steps to the square opposite the citadel ramp and enter the souk.

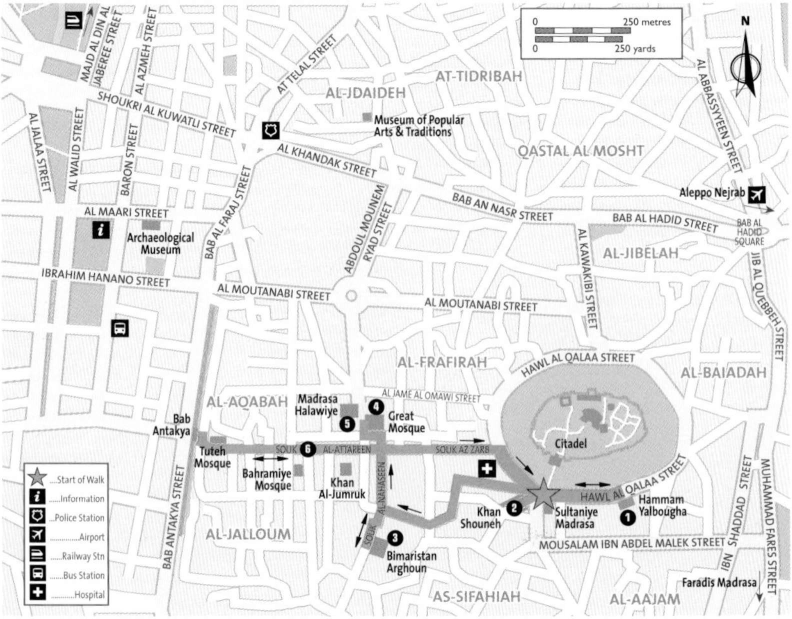

The courtyard of Aleppo's Great Mosque

2 Khan Shouneh

This is the newly restored Handicrafts Market, where an excellent range of products is on sale, from carpets to pashminas to jewellery, all at government-controlled prices. The high ceilings and space also make shopping here more relaxed than in the more claustrophobic, darker alleys of the souk proper.

At the end of the souk, follow the alley round to the left, then turn right and continue for 150m (165yds) or so to reach the Souk Al-Nahaseen (Copper-makers Market). Turn left here to reach the Bimaristan Arghoun on your left after 100m (110yds).

3 Bimaristan Arghoun

A remarkable mental hospital (*see p96*).

Retrace your steps up the Souk Al-Nahaseen for 150m (165yds) till you reach the major souk crossroads at the back of the Great Mosque. Take the first left after the crossroads, then right to find the tourist entrance.

4 Great Mosque

Aleppo's largest mosque (*see pp96–7*).

Directly opposite the mosque entrance, cross over the street into the Madrasa Halawiye.

5 Madrasa Halawiye

This fine courtyarded madrasa was formerly a cathedral (*see p97*).

Return to the souk crossroads and turn right into the main souk.

6 Souk Al-Attareen (Perfume-sellers Market)

This is the main thoroughfare of the Aleppo souks, rightly famed as the most authentic city souks left anywhere in the Middle East. In total they cover 12km (7½ miles) of winding, narrow alleys, in places retaining the original stone vaulting with holes for skylights. The smells trapped in this closed world range from wonderful perfumes and soap to the raw flesh of carcasses. Some parts date back to the 13th century, making them older by far than the bazaars of Istanbul. In the mid-18th century there were 68 flourishing *khans*, and one of the biggest, Khan Al-Jumruk, is just 20m (22yds) along to your left on the main Souk Al-Attareen thoroughfare. You can continue exploring the Souk Al-Attareen along its full length, passing the Bahramiye Mosque on your left and the Tuteh Mosque on your right, till you reach Bab Antakya (Gate of Antioch) at the far end after about 500m (550yds).

Retrace your steps along the Souk Al-Attareen to emerge at the cluster of cafés opposite the citadel ramp.

The hammam or Turkish Bath

An experience you should definitely try to incorporate into your trip is an authentic Turkish Bath, known in Arabic as a hammam. You need a spare two hours for this, as it is not something to be rushed. Men's and women's times are strictly separated, with women frequently relegated to just one or two days a week, or else day times, leaving it clear for the men in the evenings. The baths generally open from 10am till 10pm.

Aleppo is probably the best place to take a hammam, in the magnificent 14th-century Hammam Yalbougha just opposite the citadel. Also known as Hammam Al-Nasri, these grand baths were rescued from their sad fate as a felt factory in 1985 and carefully restored. In Damascus there are also a few options, of which the Hammam Nur Ed-Din (men only) and Hammam Al-Malik Az-Zaher (women Mondays only) are the best.

There is no clue from its outside appearance as to what goes on inside a hammam

Be prepared on entering the hammam to find it quite busy. Sometimes there can be upwards of 100 people inside, and it can be quite bewildering if it is your first visit. Do not be deterred, but find the person in charge and ask what the system is and say you want soap and a massage. The usual pattern is to be handed a small cotton towel along with some Aleppo soap and a coarse, straw-like rub, and told to leave your clothes somewhere on the raised seating area. Valuables such as jewellery can be put in a small locker. This first room, the changing room, is often the most beautiful architecturally, so do take time to look at the ceiling and admire it properly. Wrapped in your cotton towel after undressing, you pass through into the next room where you can start washing yourself at one of the marble basins, using the soap and rub, and

In a hammam changing room

the metal scoop to rinse yourself. Further into the hammam there will be a steam room where you can sit for as long as you like.

Once you have had your fill of the steam room, you go to find the masseur/masseuse. This is the most enjoyable part of any hammam as you put yourself totally into their hands and just relax. You will be massaged head to toe, front and back, on a huge slab usually of marble, and scrubbed with the coarse rub afterwards. Your hair and scalp will be massaged as well and the whole process usually takes 10–15 minutes. After that you can wash again and relax out in the changing area sipping tea.

SECRETS OF THE HAREM

The hammam was traditionally the venue for frank exchanges between women about the intimate secrets of their sexual practices. Lady Jane Digby, the English aristocrat who spent the last 20 years of her life in Syria married to a Bedouin sheikh (*p118*), learnt many such secrets from her weekly visits to the hammam, and passed some of them on to Richard Burton, translator of *A Thousand and One Nights* and *The Perfumed Garden*, who credited her with supplying much of his background material.

ALEPPO CITADEL

This masterpiece of medieval military architecture dominates the entire city from its almost volcano-like mound, and is the single most impressive sight in Aleppo. Partly natural and partly man-made, it is the original ancient acropolis of the Amorite capital of Halap, which is why digs are ongoing on the summit. The citadel as we see it today dates from Ayyubid and early Mameluke times (12th–13th centuries), its slopes covered with stone blocks to form a glacis (smooth slope to deter scaling) and a moat that could be flooded at will.

Most of these defences date from the time of Al-Malik Al-Zahir Ghazi, a son of Saladin, though they were later badly damaged by the Mongol invasions. His palace and state rooms were restored, notably the great throne room inside the fortified tower which makes up the gatehouse. The whole ensemble served as a stronghold against the Crusaders in northern Syria.

The magnificent gatehouse is the most visually striking aspect of the citadel, the culmination of the huge stepped ramp which leads up to it. Built on eight stone arches, it is defended by its own separate tower in which the ticket office is now housed. As you approach the main gatehouse, note the long Arabic inscription just below the machicolation boxes, which records the restorations carried out after the 1260 Mongol invasion. Make a special point of noticing the extraordinarily complex entrance itself. Immediately in front of you there is only a false door, while the real doors are tucked away to the right, two massive

The impressive gatehouse of Aleppo's citadel

The long, high wall of the citadel on its unscalable mound

iron doors covered in horseshoe and arrowhead motifs. The purpose of this device was to prevent any charging at speed. Above the entrance, carved in the archway, is a pair of intertwined serpents to ward off the enemy.

Once through these outer doors there is a succession of sharp zigzags as the ramp continues to climb upwards, again to deter charging on horseback or the use of battering rams. In the ceiling above are holes through which arrows could be fired down on the enemy or hot oil or honey poured over him.

Emerging into the daylight past the final zigzag and past the carved smiling and sad lions, you will see the ongoing excavations that have uncovered the remains of neo-Hittite temples, and further on a pair of mosques, a small hammam and a modern amphitheatre still used for performances.

Open: 9am–6pm (summer); 9am–4pm (winter). Closed: Tue (all year). Admission charge.

NOBLE PRISONERS

No Crusaders ever succeeded in breaching the defences of the mighty Aleppo citadel, but two noteworthy Crusader leaders were imprisoned here. The Count of Edessa, Jocelin II, was brought here in 1150 after having his eyes put out for refusing to give up Christianity, and thrown in the dungeon where he died nine years later. As for the adventurer Renaud de Chatillon, Prince of Antioch, he spent his last 16 years here in the dank dungeons to the right of the gatehouse, to pay for all the truce breaches he authorised and committed against Muslim pilgrims on their way to Mecca.

Drive: Sites around Aleppo

This drive takes you into some of the country's most beautiful landscapes. The villagers are friendly and you might see some Druze national costumes. Much of the drive is on quiet country roads. Take your own provisions as there is nowhere suitable to eat en route and there are many excellent picnic spots.

This drive will take a leisurely full day. The total distance is about 160km (100 miles).

Setting out from Aleppo on the main road west towards Bab Al-Hawa, the border crossing into Turkey, you will come after some 40km (25 miles) to Dana village.

1 Dana

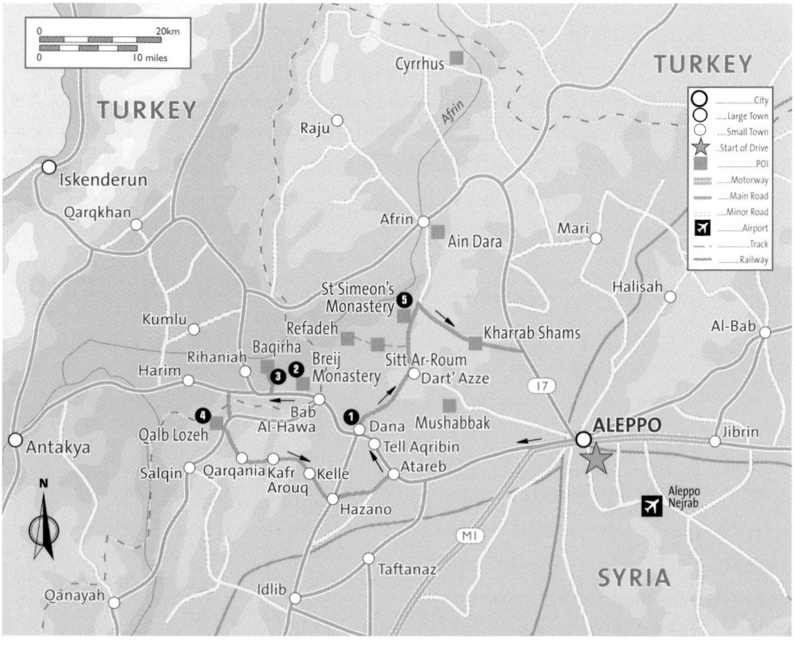

Just on the left as the main road heading through the village turns right, look out for a magnificently preserved stretch of Roman road. It heads downhill for a full 1.2 km (¾ mile) and is about 6m (20ft) wide, with fine limestone paving. It dates from the 2nd century and was restored under the French Mandate.

Follow signs to Harim, then Sarmada, and 6km (3¾ miles) further on, look out for Breij, a monastery set back about 450m (500yds) from the main road.

2 Breij Monastery

Also known as St Daniel's Monastery, this three-storey façade is well camouflaged against the rock. A Monophysite foundation and therefore heretical from the viewpoint of Byzantine Orthodoxy, it dates from the 6th century and belongs to the Syrian or Jacobite church.

Continue towards Harim and after around 3km (2 miles) fork right to Baqirha and carry on for 1.5km (1 mile).

3 Baqirha

Sitting on the ridge of this wild and rocky landscape is a striking Temple to Zeus dating from AD 161, and lower down is a series of churches and houses, some with fine stone carving.

Return to the main road and take the fork right to Qalb Lozeh, passing through a pretty valley, then take the fork left to climb 13km (8 miles) to the summit and to reach Qalb Lozeh.

4 Qalb Lozeh

This fine church is probably one of Syria's best examples of Romanesque architecture. Note its remarkable entrance façade (*see p92*).

Continue on the road to Qarqania, then Kafr Arouq, then Kelle and Hazano, then fork northeast towards Atareb. Return via Tell Aqribin to Dana, then continue through Tourmanin and Dart'Azze to St Simeon. Much of this drive will be quite slow, along small, pretty country roads. (If time is short, drive directly north to Dana from Hazano.)

5 St Simeon's Monastery

A definite highlight of this entire area, this wonderful basilica complex is best viewed in the late afternoon to enjoy the evening light after the crowds have disappeared (*see pp90–91*).

Return the 42km (26 miles) to Aleppo, following the main road to the southeast.

The Roman road at Dana

NORTH AND EAST OF ALEPPO: AIN DARA, CYRRHUS AND LAKE ASSAD

Within striking distance of Aleppo is a range of interesting and unusual sites that are worth visiting if you have a day or two to spare. From a neo-Hittite city to a Roman-Christian site and an Arab castle, all destinations listed below are well signposted and easily reached by car (*see map, p94*).

Ain Dara

Located 17km (10½ miles) north of St Simeon, so 59km (37 miles) northwest of Aleppo, this unusual site is Syria's only neo-Hittite city that still has visible remains from the 10th to the 9th centuries BC. Several small neo-Hittite kingdoms established themselves in northern Syria and southeastern Turkey, along the fringes of the Assyrian Empire, having been forced south from the cities and pastures of the Anatolian plateau, following the destruction of the Hittite Empire. The other main ones are Karatepe in southeast Turkey, and Carchemish, on the Syrian-Turkish border in a military zone.

The landscape around Ain Dara is very attractive with tree-covered hillsides and the fertile valley of the Afrin River. The ticket office sits at the foot of the hillock where the ruins are to be found, beside the houses of the Syro-Japanese excavators. The major finds were moved to the Aleppo National Museum. A five-minute climb up the grassy path takes you up onto the summit, where the approach to the temple is guarded by a solitary 3m (10ft) tall black basalt lion. The temple itself was dedicated to Ishtar, Semitic goddess of fertility, represented by a lion. She was identified in turn with the Egyptian Isis, then the Greek Aphrodite and the Roman Venus. Note especially the carved basalt blocks with sphinxes and winged lions at the entrance and the two giant footprints, each 1m (3¹/₃ft) long, on the threshold, unique in the Hittite world.

Open: 9am–6pm. Admission charge.

Cyrrhus

In a remote location right up near the Turkish border, the Roman site of Cyrrhus is 76km (47 miles) north of Aleppo. Just 1km (²/₃ mile) before the site, you have to cross a remarkable pair of very well-preserved Roman bridges, both from the 2nd century. Immediately before, the landmark for your arrival is a beautiful Roman tomb with a pyramid-shaped roof built from fine reddish stone. Set into the hillside opposite the tomb is the theatre, never excavated and heavily ruined but nevertheless impressive for its sheer size.

In Christian times, Cyrrhus was the seat of a bishopric, remaining Christian after the Muslim conquest, and the Crusaders then took it in the early 11th century. The city was finally abandoned in the late 12th century after losing its strategic role.

Open unfenced site. Free admission.

Lake Assad and Qal'at Ja'bar

Created as a result of a dam on the Euphrates in 1973, Lake Assad flooded a number of archaeological sites. One of these can still be visited, however; Qal'at Ja'bar, a 12th-century Arab castle sitting on its own mound and approached by a new causeway leading across the lake to it. The entrance is through an impressive rock-cut gateway, and inside you can enjoy a walk round the ramparts with excellent views over the lake. There is also a fine red-brick minaret and a small museum. *Open: 9am–6pm (summer); 9am–4pm (winter). Admission charge.*

A Hittite lion in Ain Dara

The Syrian coast and its hinterland

This is the Mediterranean face of Syria, closest in geography to Cyprus, with a fairly narrow coastal plain backed by high mountains forested with pine trees. Some of Syria's most beautiful scenery can be seen here, especially in spring, with foothills of gently undulating orchards of fruit trees, olive groves and tobacco plants, then rising to peaks of over 1,500m (4,920ft). High in the hills is a series of small towns and villages, such as Slounfeh, Al-Haffeh and Mashta Al-Helu, much favoured as summer retreats by Gulf Arabs escaping the heat of their own summers.

Known as the Ansariye Mountains (*see map, p116*), these hills have always formed a barrier between the coast and the interior, and the coast has, as a result, always been culturally different to the Fertile Crescent and the desert. The name Ansariye comes from ansar meaning 'disciples' in Arabic, a reference to Christians, as these mountains were traditionally home to Christian minorities. Other religious minorities have also historically sought refuge from persecution here, notably the notorious Assassins who, like the Crusaders, also built a series of mountain strongholds in the course of the 10th century to consolidate their military strength.

In ancient times, the Phoenicians founded a series of important city-states along the coast based on maritime trade in the 2nd and 1st millennia BC. Then in medieval times the Crusaders also established various strongholds here, building powerful castles strategically located in the hills to defend the coastal plain and protect the passage of Christian pilgrims on their way to Jerusalem.

Syria's 175km (110-mile) coastline does not greatly inspire swimming, except in the extreme south, near

ONCE SYRIA, NOW TURKEY

The area north of here, formerly known as the Sanjak of Alexandretta, was taken from Syria and given to Turkey by France in 1939 on the eve of World War II to ensure Turkish neutrality. With a population of over a million and including the cities of Antioch (Antakya) and Alexandretta (Iskenderun), it is now known as the Hatay Province of Turkey, though Syrian maps still show the original border.

Amrit, where a 5-star holiday complex is now under way, and in the extreme north, above Lattakia. Indeed, the coastline around Lattakia is known as Syria's Côte d'Azur, with fine sandy beaches and a few good beach hotels including a Meridien and a Sofitel, and further north the beaches are more deserted, backed by pine woods, with strange black sand giving them a very unusual quality.

The hills around Kassab up near the Turkish border constitute Syria's most beautiful mountain scenery, with hillsides covered in pine unfortunately prone, as elsewhere in the Mediterranean, to forest fires in summer. Kassab is also home to the majority of Syria's Armenian population, and Armenian churches and typical red roofs are to be seen in all the villages here.

The Syrian coast destinations below are listed in the order in which you will come to them, assuming you are travelling from the south.

The green foothills of the Ansariye Mountains

KRAK DES CHEVALIERS

Now a UNESCO World Heritage Site, this is the most spectacular and perfectly preserved Crusader castle in the world, the pinnacle of medieval military architecture. Perched up at an altitude of 750m (2,460ft), it is located to dominate and guard the so-called Homs Gap, the break in the mountains which allowed passage from the coast to the desert trade routes. Under the French Mandate, Krak was seen as a symbol of Western dominance in the Orient, so much so that the French bought it in 1933 and declared it a French monument.

The French had to dig out the millions of cubic metres of detritus accumulated over the centuries, such a monumental task that they had to call in the army's help. The 600 or so locals who had taken up residence inside also had to be moved out and relocated to the village of Qal'at Al-Husn that now sprawls below the castle.

You can drive here directly from Damascus in around 2 hours or from Hama in one hour and 45 minutes, or even, surprisingly, from Palmyra, skirting Homs, in 2 hours 30 minutes. It lies 51km (32 miles) west of Homs and 65km (40 miles) southeast of Tartous, just 15 minutes off the main dual carriageway to the coast. It is best to time your visit for early or late in the day, as Krak now receives considerable numbers of visitors, often day-trippers or coachloads of school children, all of whom arrive round the middle of the day. April is the busiest month, with Easter and the national holiday on 17 April, and the spring flowers and blossoming trees making it an attractive time, but late February/early March is also good, with cooler temperatures but fewer visitors. You should allow at least one and a half hours for a visit. The best overview from the outside is from the west, the opposite side to the entrance, where the road skirts the outer wall and passes the aqueduct. From here you can admire the massive fortification walls, the outer and the inner.

The castle

What you see today is largely unchanged since the 12th and 13th centuries. Its mighty defences were never breached, though it was laid siege to many times. It fell eventually to trickery, however, when the Mameluke Sultan Baibars arranged to have a letter sent supposedly from the Crusader commander at Tripoli, advising the knights to surrender as there were no more reinforcements. The 300 knights inside did as they were told and surrendered on condition of safe conduct to Tripoli, only to discover the letter was a forgery.

Entering over the bridge and through the magnificent ramp, the long dark passage zigzags up to reach the inner enclosure. Make sure, in addition to the obvious areas of the towers, Gothic hall, refectory, latrines and 12th-century Romanesque chapel, to explore the kitchen, the storage areas and hidden passageways behind them that emerge by the oven. Also recommended is a complete circuit of the ramparts to enjoy the views inside and out.

Simple café/restaurant facilities are available inside.

Open: 9am–6pm (summer); 9am–4pm (winter).
Admission charge.

Looking from the inner walls over the outer walls of Krak des Chevaliers

TARTOUS AND AMRIT

Both located in the southern stretch of Syria's coastal region, the area south of Tartous has some fine sandy beaches with development potential, and a 5-star holiday complex is under construction not far from Amrit. Amrit itself is a unique site, and a trip to this ancient Phoenician city is well worth the effort.

Tartous

As Syria's second port, Tartous has quite an industrial feel, though it does have a seafront with a few fish restaurants. Beyond these, its attractions are basically limited to its museum housed in the old Crusader cathedral to the north of the port. The heavily ruined citadel close by was once a Templar stronghold, now inhabited by the city's poor, and distinctly squalid to walk round.

Arwad Island

Boats run from Tartous harbour across to the island, taking about 20 minutes. The island is tiny, crowned by a Crusader fort which was the knights' last foothold in the east before they were forced to retreat to Cyprus in 1303.
Fort open: 9am–4pm. Closed: Tue.
Admission charge.

Tartous Museum

If you keep on the coast road north towards Baniyas you will come to the Crusader citadel and cathedral. The 13th-century cathedral-turned-museum still houses a 5th-century altar, along with a range of exhibits including Phoenician sarcophagi from Amrit to colourful Roman and Byzantine glass. Note its impressive external buttresses to protect against earthquakes. There are café facilities.
Open: 9am–6pm (summer); 9am–4pm (winter). Closed: Tue.
Admission charge.

Amrit

Seven kilometres (4¼ miles) south of Tartous along the road that hugs the coast, Amrit is unique in Syria, being a Phoenician city as opposed to a Hellenistic or Roman one, with its own special atmosphere. The site lies in an attractive rural setting away from any local village, with olive groves and pine trees all around. On arrival, the first monument you encounter is the extraordinary 2nd-millennium BC Phoenician temple built in the middle of a huge sunken courtyard 5.5m (18ft) deep, which would originally have been

EARLIEST ATHLETICS STADIUM

Dated to the 15th century BC, the Amrit stadium is the earliest ever stadium found, meaning that the concept of sports races like running, jumping, wrestling and throwing originated not in Greece as always claimed before, but here in Syria. Designed to hold 11,200 spectators, the stadium also has two tunnels for entry cut directly from the bedrock with steps, an amazing feat of labour.

The harbour at Tartous

filled with water from a local spring so that the temple was reachable only by boat. The temple itself is dedicated to the god Melqart, similar to the Greek Hercules and linked to Imhotep, the Egyptian god of healing. The scale and decorative style show influences from ancient Egypt and from Persia.

Follow the track 200m (220yds) over towards the line of trees and you will be rewarded with the discovery of a remarkable rock-cut stadium 220m (720ft) long by 30m (98ft) wide, almost identical dimensions to the stadium at Olympia in Greece.

Look out finally for the two tall funerary monuments 500m (550yds) away to the south of the temple, locally known as 'The Spindles', a pair of impressive carved monuments with tomb chambers below.

Open unfenced site. Free admission.

MARQAB CASTLE AND SALADIN'S CASTLE

These are the two other major Crusader castles in Syria after Krak des Chevaliers, both to be found in the Ansariye Mountains, defending their own vantage points. Both sites have simple refreshments available. Full driving directions of how to reach each castle are provided in the drive route (*see pp116–17*).

Marqab Castle

With its buildings covering the largest area of all the Crusader castles, this mighty fortress, a sombre mass of black

The view over the battlements of Saladin's Castle

basalt, sits lowering on its extinct volcano over the coastal plain, the only one of Syria's Crusader castles to overlook the sea. The name 'Marqab' means 'place of watching'. Its vast storerooms and cellars were stocked with enough provisions for 1,000 men to survive a five-year siege. Along with Krak, this was a stronghold for the Knights Hospitallers (or Knights of St John), and served as their headquarters in the 13th century.

Saladin took one look at the castle's powerful battlements and moved on, but it did eventually fall in 1285 to the Mameluke Sultan Qalaun after his forces mined the south tower. It was the last of the three great Crusader castles to fall, Krak having fallen 14 years earlier.

Inside, look out for the Great Hall of the Hospitallers, and the chapel, a beautiful early Gothic gem with elegant vaulting and simple proportions, and traces of a Last Supper fresco in a side room.

Open: 9am–6pm (summer); 9am–4pm (winter). Closed: Tue.
Admission charge.

SALADIN (1139–93)

Our Western corruption of the proper Arabic name *Salah Ad-Din* (Reformer of Religion), Saladin is the one familiar name to Westerners on the Arab side of the Crusades. In fact he was ethnically Kurdish and, despite his reputation as a great warrior, only fought when absolutely necessary, but in his lifetime he united Egypt and the Levant under Sunni (Orthodox Islam) dominance. He was merciful towards his prisoners and accumulated no personal wealth. A cultured and refined man, he patronised scholars and encouraged theological studies. His 17 sons formed a dynasty called the Ayyubids, who bequeathed much beautiful architecture in the form of mosques and madrasas, especially in Damascus, and introduced advanced water systems.

Saladin's Castle

The northernmost of the Crusader castles, 43km (27 miles) northeast of Lattakia and 160km (100 miles) from Aleppo, Sahyoun, as it is known in Arabic (French 'Saone'), sits at an altitude of 410m (1,345ft) on a dramatic, heavily wooded spur overlooking ravines to both sides. The name comes from the early Crusader knight Robert de Saone, who took over the original Byzantine fortress in 1108, living here with his son and descendants till Saladin captured it in 1188.

The castle's outer walls encompass 5 hectares (12$^1/_3$ acres), easily the largest Crusader castle in area, and twice the size of Krak. After its capture, it remained in Muslim hands, but from the 13th century it fell into obscurity. A small village grew up within its walls for a time, later abandoned. As you arrive, note especially the 28m (92ft) tall pinnacle of rock shaped like an obelisk, carved out of the solid rock to support a drawbridge, making the castle impregnable from that side.

Open: 9am–6pm (summer); 9am–4pm (winter). Closed: Tue.
Admission charge.

Drive: Crusader and Assassins' castles

Starting from a base of Hama (or Homs or Safita if you prefer), this tour of Syria's major castles of the Ansariye Mountains will take you along a mixture of dual carriageway, coastal main road and minor country roads. You will see all types of military architecture, from Byzantine to Crusader and Arab. Start off early and take food, water and a torch, as there are only simple cafés at the castles, if any at all. Avoid Tuesdays when some of them are shut.

This tour will take a full day. The total distance is about 350km (215 miles).

Set off west from Hama for 40km (25 miles), following the signposts to Masyaf.

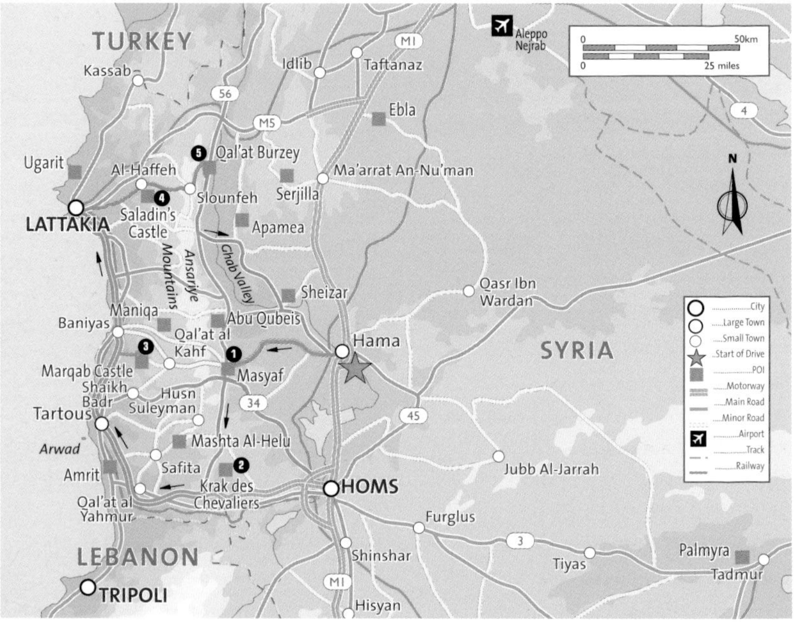

1 Masyaf

Perched on its rocky crag at the edge of the mountains, Masyaf is the largest and best preserved of the Assassins' castles, newly restored courtesy of the Agha Khan Fund.

Open: 9am–6pm (summer); 9am–4pm (winter). Admission charge.

Head south from Masyaf on the mountain road to Krak des Chevaliers, passing through Christian villages and fruit orchards.

2 Krak des Chevaliers

If you get to see just one Crusader castle in your lifetime, this should be it. A UNESCO World Heritage Site, the magnificent castle is the most stunning of its kind in the world (*see pp112–13*).

From Krak you have a choice of either heading west 30km (19 miles) through villages along small country roads to Safita, to see the keep of the Crusader castle in the centre of town, or heading south to join the main coast dual carriageway and drive northwest 65km (40 miles) to Tartous. About 43km (27 miles) north of Tartous, just south of the Baniyas exit, follow the signs to Marqab for 4km (2½ miles) of winding road.

3 Marqab Castle

Marqab is unique in offering views over the sea (*see pp114–15*).

Return to the coastal highway and continue north 60km (37 miles) to Lattakia. Follow the signs east towards Al-Haffeh, then fork right at the western end of the village, onto a small road that reaches Sahyoun Castle after 4km (2½ miles).

4 Sahyoun Castle

Saladin's Castle, as it is also called, is the largest of them all (*see pp114–15*).

Continue up into the hills to the village resort of Slounfeh and down the other side looking out for Qal'at Burzey near the bottom.

5 Qal'at Burzey

Dramatically crowning its own rocky hill at the foot of the Ansariye Mountains, this 12th-century Crusader castle was taken by Saladin in 1188. Now heavily ruined, it can only be reached by a stiff 45-minute climb.

Return south through the Ghab river valley through fertile farming land to Hama, passing the turn to Apamea (see pp78–9) en route.

THE ASSASSINS

The Assassins were an esoteric Shi'a Isma'ili sect of Islam that was founded in 1090. The name 'Assassins' comes from a corruption of the Arabic *hashish* meaning 'grass'. Their adherents were said to be drugged with *hashish*, then brainwashed and sent off on assassination missions to kill prominent opponents, with promises of paradise on return. Their power was destroyed by the Mongol warlord Hulagu in 1256, whereupon their castles fell into ruin. There were originally ten Assassins' castles in these Ansariye Mountains, but most are heavily ruined and difficult to reach.

Famous adventurers

From the 19th century onwards, Syria has attracted a succession of colourfully eccentric Westerners, all of whom felt drawn to the complexities of the Eastern way of life. Most of them went on to write about their experiences, giving us a body of travel literature whose appeal endures to this day.

Lady Jane Digby (1807–81)

This English aristocrat arrived in Syria alone in her very late 40s after a string of failed marriages and affairs that produced six children. She was forced to flee England after a scandalous divorce and numbered among her lovers the Bavarian King Ludwig I, a Greek count and a German baron. An excellent linguist, she learned Turkish and Arabic and had a courtyard house built in Damascus where she kept a menagerie of animals. She married the younger son of a Bedouin sheikh to whom she remained faithful till her death over 20 years later, spending six months each year in the desert with his tribe. She is buried in the Evangelical graveyard on the outskirts of Damascus.

Lady Jane Digby

Richard Burton (1821–90)

A prodigious linguist who learnt 25 languages and 15 other dialects, Burton was expelled from Oxford University. After a failed army career he became an explorer, searching for the source of the Nile with Speke. He next moved to the Foreign Office and became British Consul in Damascus from 1869–71. His wife Isabel's Catholic evangelising and Muslim intrigue cut short his post and he was dismissed. During his time in Damascus he became good friends

T E Lawrence in Arab garb

with Lady Jane Digby, who provided him with much of the raw material for his Eastern erotica. He went on to translate the *Kama Sutra* (1883), *The Perfumed Garden* (1886) and *The Arabian Nights* (1885–8).

Gertrude Bell (1868–1926)

Very rich but not aristocratic, Gertrude Bell was a superb linguist and travelled extensively throughout the Middle East after getting a First in History from Oxford. Dressed as a man, she studied local ruins, staying with local sheikhs, and her book *The Desert and the Sown* was the first account of such desert travels to reach a Western audience. She worked with Lawrence for British Intelligence during World War I and played a large but unrecognised part in organising the Arab Revolt.

T E Lawrence (1888–1935)

Immortalised by the film *Lawrence of Arabia*, Lawrence was the illegitimate son of an Irish aristocrat. He studied at Oxford University and in his summer holidays toured France by bicycle, making notes and taking photos of Crusader castles. In 1909 he walked about 1,600km (1,000 miles) alone in Syria exploring Crusader castles for three months for his thesis on the influence of the Crusades on European military architecture, which earned him a First-class Honours degree. He then worked as a field archaeologist on digs in Carchemish in northern Syria and elsewhere till the war broke out, when he served in Cairo with the Intelligence Staff. In the final weeks of the war he was involved in the capture of Damascus from the Ottomans and was promoted to Lieutenant-Colonel. His major work, *Seven Pillars of Wisdom*, is the record of his war experiences. He refused a CBE in 1918.

LATTAKIA AND UGARIT

From a base in Lattakia you can enjoy this northern coastline of Syria with its heavily forested hills and sandy beaches, and visit Ugarit just to the north, a fascinating and major ancient site in terms of size as well as historical and archaeological importance. But Lattakia itself is a town worth exploring; with its wide, palm-lined avenues, busy shops and street cafés, it has more of a French feel than anywhere else in the country.

Lattakia

Syria's largest Mediterranean town and main port, Lattakia doesn't really have a proper corniche, unlike Tartous to the south, but it is still a pleasant cosmopolitan place, boasting one Roman relic in the form of a fine tetrapylon which once marked the crossroads of the ancient city of Laodicea. There is also a small museum housed in an attractive Ottoman *khan* near the docks.

The beach hotels are all located about 10km (6 miles) north in the Côte d'Azur.

ALAWITE MINORITY

Syria's largest religious minority, with about 1,350,000 adherents, the Alawites are an offshoot of Shi'a Islam with some pre-Islamic and even Christian elements. They have traditionally been concentrated in the area round Lattakia and in the mountains behind, and have been growing in prosperity in recent years, heavily favoured by the ruling Assad family who are Alawites themselves. Persecuted as heretics for centuries, Iran's Ayatollah Khomeini issued a *fatwa* (religious edict) in 1979 declaring the Alawites to be within the pale of Islam, giving Assad legitimacy at a time when he was under pressure at home from the Sunni orthodoxy.

EARLIEST ALPHABET

The world's first alphabet was discovered here on clay tablets in the palace archives. The origin of the Semitic languages of Arabic and Hebrew, it has just 30 highly simplified letters each representing a phonetic sound, and was devised between 1400 and 1300 BC. Before that, the other forms of writing were Egyptian hieroglyphs and Mesopotamian cuneiform, both of which used hundreds of symbols representing whole words or syllables.

Ugarit

Known in Arabic as Ras Shamra (Headland of Fennel), Ugarit is clearly signposted 15km (9½ miles) northeast of Lattakia, on a site that was once by the sea, now 1km (2/3 mile) inland across fields. In its heyday in the 2nd millennium BC, this was one of the most major Bronze Age sites in the Middle East.

On arrival, the first aspect of the site you will see is the massive stone postern gateway into the city, similar in design to the early Mycenaean gateways of Greece. Its steps lead up into the 90-roomed Royal Palace and near the top was a loose stone that could be pushed out to make a peephole for spying on the path from the harbour to the palace. Today the modern entrance is via the ticket office on a raised mound, and your first reaction on entering may be disappointment. Persist, however, and you will be rewarded with a remarkable sense, after further exploration, of the sheer scale and grandeur of this site and especially the palace. Notice in particular the amazingly advanced water system, with wells, channels and basins everywhere, the Royal Tombs, and the House of Rapanou, a 34-room villa complete with the owner's underground mausoleum.

Simple café facilities are on site. *Open: 9am–6pm (summer); 9am–4pm (winter). Admission charge.*

The entrance to the Bronze Age Royal Palace at Ugarit

Getting away from it all

Of all of Syria's sites, the most visited outside Damascus and Aleppo are without doubt Palmyra and Krak des Chevaliers, although even these are hardly crowded by Western standards. However, for those who crave real solitude and quiet, the country offers many sites that give the chance to escape such crowds as there are. The following are just a selection.

Assassins' castles

The largest and most accessible of these is at Masyaf (*see p117*). Of the string of ten that existed at the height of the Assassins' power in the 12th century, the only other ones worth visiting now are Al-Kahf, Abu Qubeis and Maniqa. Qal'at Al-Kahf (Castle of the Cave) is the most dramatic, perched on a ridge between two gorges. It lies 8km (5 miles) southeast of Marqab Castle and is best approached from Shaikh Badr, driving north 4km (2½ miles) to Ain Breisin, then 7km (4¼ miles) to Al-Nmreije, the nearest village. From here a driveable track runs the last 2km (1¼ miles) to the castle. The excursion takes a whole day from either Tartous or Krak, and the roads are winding and tortuous.

Open sites. Free admission.

Husn Suleyman

One of the remotest sites in Syria, this extraordinary, gigantic temple dating from the 1st century sits high in the mountains north of Krak des Chevaliers. Well worth the effort, it can be reached either from Safita (25km/15½ miles) or from Masyaf or from Krak des Chevaliers itself. As the route is not signposted nor straightforward, the following directions may be helpful:

From Safita, begin by heading north and just on the edge of town (around 500m/550yds from the centre) fork right and continue for 20km (12½ miles), then turn left and continue for 3km (1¾ miles) to reach the village of Husn Suleyman. From here you need to ask.

From Krak, the drive takes 90 minutes and you start by heading north towards Masyaf, passing through rural Christian villages. At a major junction at which Masyaf is marked 15km (9½ miles) to the right, you turn left towards Tartous and Dreikish. This road climbs up through thickly wooded slopes and at the top your landmark is the three television masts in the distance; the site lies immediately below these, to the right in a small valley.

Roughly contemporary with Baalbek in Lebanon, the massive temple nestles in a natural rocky amphitheatre, within a compound measuring 134m by 85m (440ft by 280ft), entered by four impressive gateways, each with an eagle carved on the underneath of its lintel. Some of its grey stone blocks are over 10m (33ft) long. It can be cold and windy at this altitude especially in the winter and spring months, so come prepared, and bring a picnic as there are no facilities.

Open unfenced site.
Free admission.

Mushannaf

Set in the remote hills of the Jebel Druze right in the south of Syria in the tiny village of Mushannaf east of Suweida and northeast of Salkhad (*see pp53–4 and map, p29*), lies this rarely visited little gem of a Roman temple built beside an artificial lake. Dated by an inscription to AD 171, the temple stands to the right of the road as you enter the village of Mushannaf from Salkhad in the south, immediately after crossing a bridge. The local washerwoman has taken up residence in the Holy of Holies, her giant cauldron occupying the space where the altar would once have been, and her goats run round in front of the beautifully carved façade of the temple with its Corinthian capitals and rosette motifs.
Free admission.

Qal'at Najm

Difficult to incorporate into any itinerary because it lies by itself on a rocky crag overlooking the Euphrates 90km (56 miles) northeast of Aleppo, this 13th-century Arab castle is rarely visited, making it a perfect excursion for getting off the beaten track. You will

The 1st-century temple of Husn Suleyman

have to come with your own car or hired taxi as there is no public transport, and there are no facilities in the area so come well provisioned.

Its name means 'Castle of the Star' and the surrounding scenery is very fine. It was largely the work of the Ayyubid governor of Aleppo and son of Saladin, Al-Malik Al-Zahir Ghazi, between 1208 and 1215. Recently restored by the Antiquities Department, the castle suffered heavy damage under the Mongol invasions in the late 13th and 14th centuries. After the citadel in Aleppo, it represents the next best example of Arab fortification techniques, with many underground rooms and passageways. Bring a torch to explore the darker recesses.

To get there, from Aleppo head towards Ar-Raqqa, then turn left at the airport junction on the new road to the Al-Jezira region. After 71km (44 miles) you reach Membij; continue 17km (10½ miles), crossing the new bridge over the Euphrates, then turn right (southeast) and continue for 3km (1¾ miles) to the castle.

Qal'at Yahmur

Just 10km (6¼ miles) southeast from Tartous, this small Crusader castle makes a short detour off the main highway, if you find yourself with an hour to spare. Look out for a green signpost off the main dual carriageway marked Qal'at Al-Uraymah, and follow the small road for 2km (1¼ miles) to reach the village where the unmistakeable honey-coloured stone building rises above the low-rise houses.

Like a miniature keep, the charming castle was known by the Crusader knights as Chastel Rouge from the colour of its stone. Originally a 10th-century Byzantine fort, the Hospitallers carried out extensive modifications in 1177. It was taken briefly by Saladin but later captured back by the Crusaders, before falling in 1289 to the Mameluke Sultan Qalaun.

The guardian and his family now inhabit the castle but will be delighted to show you round and take you up onto the roof. There are no set times or entry fee, but a small tip is always appreciated for their time and trouble.

Qasr Ibn Wardan

Lying by itself in the desert 58km (36 miles) northeast of Hama, this unusual Byzantine church and palace is reached by a 40-minute drive from the Hama Museum on the northern outskirts of town. It is signposted from there. You should have at least two full hours spare to make this detour, as it cannot be incorporated into any circuit and you have to return to Hama before continuing on to anywhere else.

Unique in Syria, Qasr Ibn Wardan was built as a defensive palace to guard against the threat from Persia in the east and at the same time to control the Arab nomadic population. Its distinctive striped appearance comes from the use of alternating black basalt with yellow

The remains of the church at Qasr Ibn Wardan, erected in the mid-6th century by the Byzantine Emperor Justinian I

Quneitra is now abandoned and patrolled by UN soldiers

brick, and its elegant shapes stand out against the flat and barren desert landscape from afar as you approach.

The largest part of the complex is the palace, still standing to two storeys high. The governor would have lived here. Note the kitchen areas with their olive presses, wells and basalt grinding stones. The church lies to the left of the palace and also has steps leading up to the second storey. The brick dome, originally 20m (66ft) high, was the only baked-brick dome found anywhere in Syria.

The guardian lives nearby and will come soon after your arrival to unlock the buildings.

Open: 9am–6pm (summer); 9am–4pm (winter). Admission charge.

Quneitra

Rarely visited because of the complex formalities of obtaining the special pass, Quneitra guarantees you a place away from the crowds and is the only visitable place in the Golan Heights.

The road to Quneitra (50km/31 miles southwest of Damascus) skirts the eastern edge of the Anti-Lebanon Range, dominated by the often snow-covered peak of Mount Hermon at 2,814m (9,232ft). There are a couple of roadblock checks where you will have to show your pass, and for the visit itself you will be accompanied by a soldier throughout.

The Golan, lying east and north of the Sea of Galilee (Lake Tiberias), was taken by Israel in the 1967 War, since when Israel has followed its policy of building Jewish settlements there. In 1973 Egypt and Syria attempted to win it back, but after sporadic fighting, the current UN buffer zone was established and Quneitra was returned, although not before the Israeli forces flattened it with bulldozers in a gratuitous act of violence. The rest of the Golan remains firmly in Israeli hands, a situation they are keen to perpetuate as its snow-covered mountains feed Israel's largest reservoir, the Sea of Galilee, with its meltwaters. Some 15,000 Syrians still live in the Golan, mainly Druze, under Israeli occupation, largely forgotten by the international community.

The bulldozed town has an eerie feel as you drive round the network of flattened remains. Still recognisable are an Orthodox church tower, a mosque and a hospital, all punctuated with large numbers of UN personnel in blue berets.

There is a restaurant on site which offers simple meals.

Free admission.

ACCESS FORMALITIES

A special pass must be applied for which is valid only for the same day or the next day, obtainable free of charge from a special department of the Ministry of the Interior which deals with passes for foreigners. It lies in a northwest suburb of Damascus. Any taxi driver will be able to take you there. You must take your passport and hand it in at the little kiosk outside. You then wait outside for 15 minutes or so while the procedures are completed and your passport and pass are handed back.

Wildlife

There has been little systematic fieldwork on the wildlife of Syria, but it is clear from the mosaics which have come down to us from Roman times, decorating the floors of wealthy villas, that the countryside used to be home to such creatures as bears, deer, boar, wolves, hyenas and polecats. Today most of the larger animals are simply livestock, such as camels, horses, cows, donkeys, sheep, goats and poultry, the more exotic creatures having been hunted to extinction many years ago.

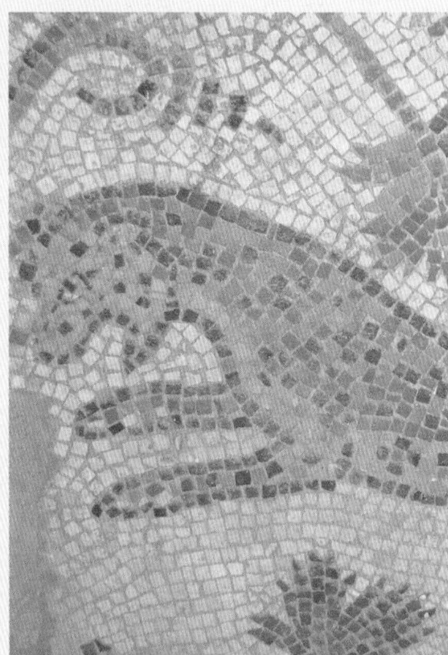

Roman mosaics reveal that wild animals were once plentiful in Syria

One particular species associated with Syria is the Syrian golden hamster. In 1930 a pregnant female was caught near Aleppo and sent back to Britain. Her offspring were the source of all our subsequent generations of hamsters.

Conservation

The whole concept of wildlife conservation is still in its infancy in Syria, but there are a handful of wildlife reserves devoted to breeding programmes, notably for oryx and gazelle, to reintroduce previously near extinct species.

Financed jointly by the Italian government, the World Food and Agriculture Organisation and the Syrian Ministry of Agriculture, the **Talila Reserve** was the first wildlife project to be launched in the country in 1992. Lying 35km (22 miles) southeast of Palmyra and clearly marked off the Deir Ez-Zour road, the reserve can be visited by making an appointment via the yellow-signed 'Range Rehabilitation' office in Tadmur, Palmyra. It has some 380 gazelle and 65 oryx within its 72km (45-mile) perimeter fence. The reserve also has a fascinating visitors' centre explaining traditional Bedouin wisdom

Turtles can be found in some courtyard fountains

on the approach to animals, nature and life in general.

Talila Reserve. Open: 9am–5pm. Free admission.

Birdlife

There are a handful of birdwatching tours that specialise in Syria, but if walking and trekking holidays manage gradually to become established in the Syrian mountains, there may be scope for more tours to develop. There are reckoned to be around 380 species in 47 families here, around 12 of which are globally threatened. The largest numbers are concentrated in the Ansariye range where the rare Syrian woodpecker, Syrian serin and crimson-winged finch are to be found, then in the Euphrates Valley and then in the seasonal salt lakes in the desert around Palmyra, which attract migrants like flamingos. Other rare birds include the desert finch, Houbara bustard, the sand partridge, imperial eagle, great bustard and bald ibis.

The commonest species of bird are doves and pigeons, found in the cities, especially Damascus. Protected by Islamic tradition, the palm doves which live in Damascus are remarkably tame and fearless, nesting regularly in the courtyard houses. They are recognisable from the black cluster of spots round their necks and their russet-coloured bodies. Reputedly responsible for a murder a week (by owners accusing each other of luring birds to their own rival rooftop coops), they form the subject of a new book by Marius Kociejowski, *The Pigeon Wars of Damascus*.

NO PETS PLEASE

Syrians, like all Arabs, do not have a pet-keeping culture, since they do not share our sentimental love for animals and our desire for animal companionship. A man may develop a relationship of respect with his horse, his camel or his falcon, but cats, dogs and hamsters do not enter the equation. An animal is kept for a purpose, such as food or breeding. A canary may be kept for its song.

When to go

Syria offers a range of different seasons to suit the requirements and preferences of different visitors, depending on who they are and where they come from. Westerners from Europe and the United States tend to favour spring and autumn when temperatures range from the low to high 20s°C (68–84°F), while Arabs favour the hotter summer. Winter is the quietest time, when the wind and rain deter most visitors.

Summer

As the northernmost and therefore coolest Arab country, Syria has long attracted large numbers of Arab visitors from the Gulf who come in the summer months to escape the searing heat of their own countries. High season for Arab tourists is therefore from mid-June, when the schools finish, to late August/early September when the schools go back. Flights into and out of Syria on Syrian Air get heavily booked over this period despite the high fares, with expatriate Syrians returning to visit their families, so if you want to travel then, you will be well advised to book by April at the latest to secure your preferred dates.

This influx of visitors puts strain on accommodation in Damascus, Aleppo and above all in the mountain summer resorts like Slounfeh, Mashta Al-Helu and Kassab, but sites like Palmyra and Bosra are largely ignored, making them relatively empty over the summer months, so room prices drop accordingly. If therefore as a Westerner you can cope with high temperatures of 35°C to 40°C (95°F to 104°F), it can be a good time to visit Palmyra and the desert sites of the Euphrates Valley, for example, as long as you have air-conditioned transport and explore the sites early morning or late afternoon. Sunset is not until 8pm in high summer, so evening daylight hours are long.

Spring and autumn

The most popular times for European and American visitors are the spring (mid-March to late May) and the autumn (mid-September to late October). Airfares at these times tend to be on the high side, though not as high as in the summer months, and accommodation prices also increase to reflect the increased demand. A surprising amount of rain can still fall in March and April, and sometimes even in May, so if you want to be sure of dry weather with lots of sunshine then late September and early October are a better bet. The UV strength of the sun will also be less then, so your chances of getting burnt diminish. Be aware that in 2008 Ramadan will fall in September and in 2009 it will fall in mid-August.

Winter

Low season is without doubt the winter months of mid-November until the end of February, with seasonal blips for Christmas and New Year when prices rise briefly again. Temperatures can drop as low as 2°C (36°F) at night and not get above 12°C (54°F) during the day, though some winter days in the desert can be wonderfully clear and crisp with excellent visibility, good for photography. Daylight hours are very short in winter, with sunrise at 6.30am and sunset as early as 4.20pm in December, meaning your itinerary has to be carefully planned to make sure you are not travelling too much in the dark.

In summer, rooftop eating is the norm

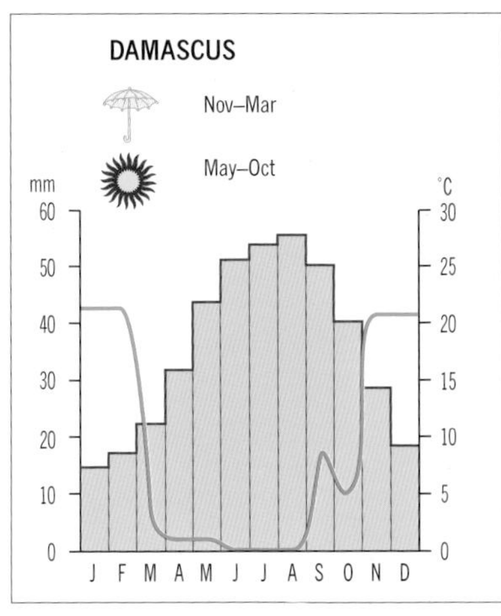

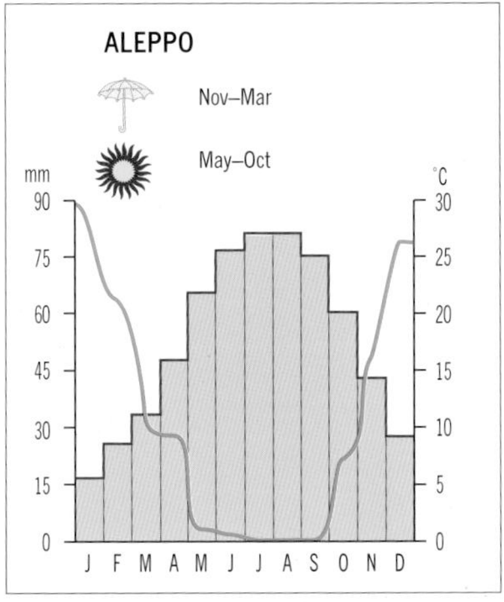

WEATHER CONVERSION CHART

25.4mm = 1 inch

°F = 1.8 × °C + 32

Getting around

The public transport network within Syria is surprisingly good, but as a visitor with limited time, the best way to travel is by car, or if you have more time at your disposal, by luxury bus. The train service is extremely limited and slow, with the exception of the Damascus-Aleppo commuter link. Internal air links work well between Damascus, Aleppo, Lattakia and Deir Ez-Zour. Local people tend to use the buses for intercity travel and the microbuses for shorter distances in and around cities.

Intercity travel

Air

Syrian Air (*www.syriaair.com*) runs cheap domestic flights from Damascus and Aleppo to Lattakia and Deir Ez-Zour. Between Damascus and Aleppo there are up to ten flights a day, costing around SYP1,000 one-way.

Car hire and driving

Do not be daunted by the prospect of self-drive car hire in Syria as traffic is relatively well behaved by Middle Eastern standards, certainly no worse than in Italy or Portugal and nothing like as fast. The minimum age is 23 and your national driving licence is the only documentation you need. Petrol is cheap and diesel even cheaper, though take care to fill up before your tank gets below quarter full in rural areas, as petrol stations can be randomly located. The best companies are **Hertz/Chamcar** (*Tel: (011) 2232300. www.hertz.com*) or **Europcar** (*Tel: (011) 2229200. www.europcar.com*) and the cost is around US$50 a day with a minimum of three days' hire. If you only want to hire a car for one day you will have to take a chauffeur-driven one, for which the cost is closer to US$140 a day, though this includes petrol. You do not have to bear the costs of your driver's food or accommodation.

Deluxe buses

By far the best and most efficient way to travel, if you are on a limited budget, is the excellent and punctual network of deluxe coaches/buses. There are several different competing companies, though there is very little to choose between them in price or comfort, so it usually comes down to a choice based on which timings suit you best. **Qadmous**, **Al-Ahlia** and **Karnak** are three of the major ones, running all over the country. All are air-conditioned, clean and comfortable, usually offering a free fizzy drink or juice and sweets.

To get information or bookings, you have to visit one of the two Damascus bus stations in person; both are well known by locals and taxi drivers. **Baramkeh** near the Old City is for all destinations to the south and west, including Bosra, Beirut and Amman, while the **Pullman/Harasta** station is inconveniently located 5km (3 miles) northeast of the city centre just off the main Aleppo road, and offers all destinations north and east including Palmyra, Deir Ez-Zour, Tartous, Lattakia and Aleppo, as well as Turkey. Each city has its own bus

A map of the Syrian rail network

station, but Damascus is the hub. Tickets can usually be bought on the spot without a problem, though at peak holiday times and weekends it may be advisable to book in advance. Fares are very cheap, so the three-hour journey from Damascus to Amman, for example, with the excellent new company called Challenge, costs just SYP650 return. All long-distance buses break the journey for regular loo stops and leg stretching at cafés/restaurants along the way, where snacks and refreshments can be bought. Damascus to Aleppo takes five hours, Damascus to Palmyra three hours and Damascus to Amman about four hours including the border crossing.

Trains

The railway system is very slow and limited in its timetable, so is not widely used except for commercial traffic. One exception is the commuter service between Damascus and Aleppo, which, since the arrival of new diesel trains from Korea, is much smoother and more reliable.

Aleppo Station. 3km (2 miles) northwest of the city centre. www.cfssyria.org

Damascus Kadem Station. 3km (2 miles) southwest of the city centre. www.cfssyria.org

Damascus traffic can be busy, but there are always plenty of taxis

Within cities

Traffic is congested, especially in Damascus, and getting worse. It used to be very expensive for Syrians to buy cars, resulting in a natural limit to the numbers of vehicles on the road, but since import duty on vehicles was dramatically cut in 2006, more local people find themselves able to afford cars and some estimates say vehicle numbers have increased by as much as 40 per cent as a result. Parking is extremely difficult, especially in the old centres like the Old City of Damascus, where streets are very narrow. Traffic police are in evidence, though the phenomenon of clamping has yet to come to Syria. Parking tickets do not exist, though on-the-spot fines can be levied. As a foreigner many of your parking and driving offences will be overlooked.

Damascus International Airport to the city

In an attempt to regulate taxi travel between the airport and the city, a system was introduced in 2007 whereby all arriving passengers have to go to the taxi desk on emerging from customs into the arrivals hall and pre-pay for a taxi (SYP600 at the time of writing). Your destination is noted and written on a ticket which you are given, and you then wait outside for a few minutes until the next car in the taxi queuing system comes forward to pick you up. Yellow taxis are therefore totally banned from taking passengers into the city, though of course you can still catch yellow taxis to get out to the airport, for which the standard fare is SYP500. The cheaper alternative is to catch the airport bus from the airport terminal into the centre, which leaves every 30 minutes or so, but you then have to catch a yellow taxi to your final destination within the city.

Microbuses

From Baramkeh bus station in the centre of Damascus, microbuses (white minibuses seating about ten people) run to all local destinations in and around the suburbs, even as far as Zabadani in the mountains to the west, a 45-minute journey. Fares are very cheap and bought on board, and the microbuses can be hailed anywhere along their route.

Taxis

Yellow taxis are everywhere in the cities. They are heavily relied on by locals, especially women, and are very cheap as a result. Within Damascus the typical fare anywhere fairly central is SYP50, and will only creep up to SYP100 if you are headed further afield to the suburbs. A taxi up to Jebel Qassioun above the city will cost SYP200–300 each way, though locals will pay less. Meters are a rarity in taxis and functioning meters even rarer. Almost no taxis have functioning rear seat belts and many are very scruffy with broken seats and rear window handles.

Accommodation

Syria offers the full range of accommodation from top 5-star deluxe hotels right through to basic 1-star places suitable for backpackers. There are no official campsites or youth hostels. Where the country is perhaps underserved is in the middle category of 3-star places. Most hotels are concentrated in the cities and larger towns, and in the smaller towns and countryside there is virtually no accommodation of tourist standard, with the notable exception of Palmyra.

It is important to remember that in summer there is an acute shortage of accommodation in Damascus, so tourists are strongly advised to book ahead if visiting at this time. There are plans to build more hotels, especially in the coastal areas, though many of these are designed as apartment-style hotels for visiting Gulf families to stay in over the summer. In terms of numbers and spend, these account for more than any other category of tourist.

Staying with families is not usually an option because of single men not being allowed to stay in Muslim households where there are women, and single women not being allowed where there are men in the household.

BOUTIQUE HOTELS

A growing trend in Syria is for small hotels opening up in restored 18th- and 19th-century houses in the cities. On average they only offer 8 to 20 rooms and each room will be different as in any private house. Many do not have a dining room and only offer bed and breakfast, but all tend to be centrally located in the cities, so there are always plenty of restaurants nearby to choose from. Damascus and Aleppo have the most boutique hotels, and the numbers are likely to increase year by year, as they are very popular with Westerners in search of more individual accommodation offering something like an authentically traditional experience. Designed round a courtyard with central fountain and roof terraces, most are rated 3- or 4-star with en-suite bathrooms and traditional furnishings.

Five-star hotels

There are a surprising number of 5-star deluxe-category hotels, such as the Meridien, the Sheraton, the Semiramis and the Four Seasons. Damascus has the highest concentration, followed by Aleppo, then Palmyra, then Lattakia. In addition to the international chains there is also the Syrian chain of Cham Palace hotels, owned by the Syrian millionaire and benefactor Osmane Aidi. As well as the hotels, he also owns

Chamcar (affiliated with Hertz) and Cham Tour, a travel agency.

The deluxe hotels boast the usual range of facilities like swimming pools, gyms, health clubs, tennis courts and restaurants, and they can be surprisingly good value, often offering discounts, especially when booked in advance and at low season. Many of the larger chains can be booked online.

Middle category and below

There is something of a dearth of 3-star and lower 4-star hotels in Syria. A handful can be found in Damascus, Aleppo and Palmyra and then in the smaller towns like Hama and Tartous. None is very exciting or inspired. In the 2- and 1-star range, most are frequented by backpackers and students on a tight budget. Hygiene can be dubious.

The courtyard of the Beit Al-Mamlouka Hotel (*see p161*)

Food and drink

Another surprise in store for first-time visitors to Syria is the quality of the food. Syrian cuisine has an illustrious past and tradition, showing influences from both its Lebanese and its Ottoman heritage. Syrians enjoy their food and eating out forms a very important part of local culture and socialising. All age groups indulge, from grandparents to the very young, and groups of young women, usually in a mix between Western and Muslim dress, meet up in cafés and restaurants to chat and gossip, often enjoying a narghile *or water pipe together.*

The country is self-sufficient and grows all its own produce, so the quality of fruit and vegetables is excellent, generally better than your local supermarket at home, where food will have been flown in from all corners of the globe. Bananas are a notable exception, and are imported from Ecuador.

Where to eat

All cities are well provided with restaurants at every level. On any package tour you will inevitably be sucked into eating your main meals in the hotel, and these can be very uninspired and give you a false impression of what is available. The bigger hotels go in for larger, buffet-style spreads which can also be rather bland, though they usually make an attempt to offer some local specialities. Generally the 5-star hotel restaurants are used by upmarket tour groups and by visiting businessmen. Foreign food restaurants such as Chinese or Italian are rare and tend only to exist within the 5-star hotels. Local people would not dream of eating there, but will instead frequent the smaller, independent restaurants of high quality

SYRIAN SPECIALITIES

Baba ghanouj chunky aubergine dip with olive oil
Fataayer/borek fine pastries in triangles or cigar shapes filled with cheese or spinach
Kebab halabi lamb kebab served between flat Arabic bread in a tomato sauce
Kibbeh minced lamb with onion and pine nuts, deep-fried in balls
Moutabbal aubergine dip blended smooth with sesame paste
Muhammara walnut paste mixed with hot chilli pepper
Shish taouk light main course of chicken flavoured with spices on a kebab skewer
Tabbouleh a refreshing salad of finely chopped tomatoes, mint and onion, mixed with cracked wheat

which are scattered about the city centres and in the wealthier suburbs. The menus offer an extraordinary range, usually with upwards of 15 starters and upwards of 15 main courses.

Local specialities

All meals tend to begin with *mezze*, a selection of starters, hot or cold, offering a huge variety of flavours and textures, followed by simpler main courses based round chicken and lamb. Beef is rarer. Despite the Mediterranean coastline, sea fish is expensive in Syria and not always that fresh, though the river fish from the Orontes and the Euphrates are recommended if you are staying in those vicinities.

Desserts are generally fresh fruit, often served gratis after the meal, or sticky pastries based round pistachio and soaked in honey, reminiscent of Greek *baklava*.

Fresh produce is of a very high standard

Tipping etiquette

The usual practice among Syrians is to round up the bill slightly, something around 5 per cent. A service charge is not ordinarily added to the bill except in the big, fancy 5-star hotel restaurants, and the normal view is to leave it to the discretion of the diner. Heavy tipping is to be avoided as it runs counter to the local culture.

Vegetarians

Being vegetarian in Syria is easy, as so many of the dishes, especially the starters, are based round vegetables, pulses and salads. Olives and olive oil are liberally used in everything, and

The Elissar Restaurant, in a restored house in Old Damascus, was one of the first to be established (*see pp164–5*)

ALCOHOL

Syria is far from being a 'dry' country. It even produces its own – admittedly not very good – wine, beer and *'araq*. Local people will volunteer that Lebanese wine is far superior, and it is in fact surprisingly difficult to find Syrian wine served in restaurants. The same often applies to the beer and to the *'araq*, where it is the Lebanese and Egyptian makes that are served in preference, even though they are more expensive. Hotel restaurants and bars all serve alcohol freely and the national carrier, Syrian Air, serves whisky and beer on request gratis on its flights. Restaurants that are close to mosques frequently do not serve alcohol, but those in the Christian quarters of towns and cities will always offer it. In shops in the Christian areas, wine, spirits and beer can all be bought, both local and imported varieties from Lebanon and Egypt, at very cheap prices.

there are always omelettes for main courses. Cheese is a bit more limited, and does not figure much on menus, though there are several varieties of local white cheese you can buy in little food shops, along with the excellent local yoghurt (*laban*). Nuts (especially pistachio, almond, walnut and peanut) and seeds are available in abundance from the local markets, bought loose by the 100g (3½oz). The local flat bread comes in small brown roundels or large white roundels, and there are also some speciality breads flavoured with herbs like *za'atar* (cumin) or black poppy seeds.

Fast food

The commonest Syrian fast food sold from street stalls is *falafel*, hot chickpea balls stuffed into Arab pitta bread with salad, very good for vegetarians. For meat-eaters there is *shawarma*, thinly sliced lamb or chicken from a revolving spit like the Turkish *doner* kebab, again stuffed into bread with salad. As it is freshly prepared, food is always safe to eat from these stalls.

Food shopping

This will be a totally different experience to what you may be used to in the West, as Syria is still mercifully free of supermarkets. One or two exist in Damascus in the modern outskirts where the first shopping malls to hit the country are to be found. Local people therefore shop for food in lots of little shops in the town centres.

For picnics you will find small shops selling provisions like processed cheese (the ubiquitous *La Vache Qui Rit*), fresh local white cheese, olives, natural yoghurt, jam, tea and coffee. For bread you can go directly to the baker and buy fresh from the oven, and fruit and vegetables will be on display openly in the food markets so you can pick and choose whatever looks best and freshest. Locals buy in quantity, a minimum of three kilos (6½lb) of tomatoes, for example, but that does not mean you cannot buy a quarter kilo if you want. Nuts and dried fruit also make excellent picnic and snack foods as they do not go off or mind getting squashed.

The café at St Simeon's Monastery

'Araq

An excellent accompaniment to the local food, especially if you are eating lamb, is the locally made aniseed spirit *'araq*, similar to the Greek *ouzo* and Turkish *raki*, but smoother. Like them, it goes cloudy when water is added and is normally drunk with ice and water. As with the wine, the Lebanese varieties are considered superior, though the Golan makes excellent *'araq* flavoured with cherry. Prices are very cheap and it is cheaper to drink *'araq* with your meal than wine.

Beer

The local Barada beer is named after the river that flows through Damascus and is a refreshing Pils type of pale beer with a variable alcohol content. More widely available are the various Lebanese and Egyptian beers such as Al-Maza, as well as regional versions of Stella and Heineken brewed under licence. Prices are reasonable at around SYP100–200.

Juices

A Syrian speciality is the wonderful fresh fruit juices served in restaurants, especially those not serving alcohol. Lemon with mint is a particular favourite, but there are also juices with strawberry, mango, passion fruit and banana, blended to be rather like smoothies. On the street in cities in summer you will find juice stalls squeezing fresh oranges, and the delicious fresh mulberries (Arabic *toot*) in August.

Soft drinks

The usual range of Coca-Cola and Seven Up is around, as well as local versions of Coke, lemonade and orangeade. Sometimes the diet versions are available but not consistently.

Tea and coffee

Locals drink black tea in small glasses, usually heavily sugared, in between meals and after meals. Mint tea is popular as a *digestif*, as is flower tea, known as *zuhoor*. Arabic or Turkish coffee is also drunk black in tiny cups and can be ordered *sukkar kateer* (lots of sugar), *mutawassit* (medium sugar) and *saadeh* (no sugar). Less common and usually reserved for special occasions is the clear, greenish, thin cardamom coffee as drunk by the

Bedouin. It's poured from the long-spouted brass coffee pots as opposed to the short-handled stainless-steel Turkish coffee pots put directly on the stove for heating.

Wines

The local Syrian wine is usually St Simeon, available in red or white, and rated inferior to Lebanese wines such as Ksara Reserve or Chateau Kefraya. If you can find Syrian wine on the menu it generally sells for SYP800 in restaurants, while the Lebanese wines are in the SYP1,000–1,400 range. There is not usually much of a choice, just three or four if you are lucky.

Blanc de Blancs is one of the best white wines available in Syria

Entertainment, sport and leisure

This section is very short for the simple reason that there is very little in the way of entertainment in Syria. Eating out is the main recreation for local people, who see socialising together with friends or family over a meal and a shared narghile *(water pipe or hubbly bubbly) as the most enjoyable way to spend leisure time. There is virtually no drinking culture, with hardly any bars even in Damascus, though men will gather to sit and chat over tea and coffee in the street cafés.*

Cultural entertainment

Damascus boasts as its cultural venue the Dar Al-Assad, an impressive modern opera house, and the excellent Syrian National Symphony Orchestra which performs there regularly.

Otherwise, all cultural performances are organised by the foreign cultural institutes like the Goethe Institut, the Institut Français or the British Council. All performances are listed in the English daily paper, the *Syria Times*.

OUR FOOD AND DRINK DEBT

Of all the surprising things we owe to the Arab world, the most surprising is probably alcohol, Arabic *al-kuhool*. The distillation process was invented around 800 by Islam's foremost scientist Jabir Ibn Hayyan, though drinking the product was cautioned against in the Koran. The concept of the three-course meal, with soup followed by fish or meat, then fruit and nuts, was brought by an Iraqi to Spain in the 9th century. Coffee also came to us from the Arabian Peninsula, via Syria and Turkey to Venice, and a Turk opened the first coffee house in London in 1650. The Arabic word *qahwa* became the Turkish *kahve*, then the Italian *caffè* and then the English coffee. Arabic *sukkar* has also given us English sugar.

Nightlife

No one comes to Syria for the nightlife. That said, the 5-star hotels usually have a nightclub of some sort, and a few restaurants in the big cities like Damascus and Aleppo have some live shows with music and even the occasional whirling dervish, usually starting after 10pm. Cinemas are in short supply and tend to offer a staple diet of B-grade Western movies favouring martial arts and screaming women.

Sport and leisure

As everywhere in the Middle East, football is the national sport, played everywhere and anywhere on whatever scrap of ground can be found. Actual sports facilities are extremely limited, however, and are concentrated in the 5-star hotels where swimming pools, tennis courts and fitness centres are usually on offer. Golf is in its infancy with just a handful of courses attached to the big hotels. The beach hotels offer waterskiing, windsurfing and pedaloes, and maybe a bit of volleyball.

Horse riding and camel trekking tours can be set up in advance through certain specialist tour operators, and some specialist guides are able to offer walking and hiking tours in the mountain or desert.

Jasmin Tours Syria. PO Box 12353, Damascus. Tel: (011) 231 3176. Email: jasmin@jasmintours.com

Ancient bicycles are well used in the cities by locals weaving in and out of the traffic and to speed up progress in narrow alleyways not open to vehicle traffic. Serious cycling with helmets and modern gear has yet to arrive in Syria.

The swimming pool at the Talisman Hotel in the Jewish Quarter of Damascus

Shopping

Syria offers an excellent variety of good-quality souvenirs, many of which are still made by local craftsmen. Prices are very reasonable by Western standards. The souks or Arab markets are the best places to buy, located in the old city centres particularly of Damascus and Aleppo, both of which have a specially designated handicrafts market where prices are fixed. In Damascus this is the area round the Suleymaniye Tekke complex not far from the National Museum, and in Aleppo it is in Souk Ash-Shouneh, just at the beginning of the main souks opposite the citadel. The quality of the goods in these souks is high and geared to Western tastes.

Cloth

Damascus is famous for its damask cloth, and the fine quality of its materials and weaves in general. Tablecloths and matching napkins are an excellent-value purchase, available in all colours and embroidered in gold or silver. There are also pashminas in beautiful colours and designs, useful as shawls or just as throws. Silk scarves are an Aleppo speciality.

BARGAINING

All the locals bargain and it is simply part of the shopping process. As a foreigner the starting price will generally be higher, but you should counter with a lower offer, aiming to shave at least 20 per cent off. The best technique is never to show interest in the item you actually want, and in fact you will always get your best bargains on something you genuinely didn't want, but the price came down so far you couldn't resist it anyway. In some souks, like the handicraft markets in Damascus and Aleppo where prices are government controlled, there is very little scope for bargaining, and some stall owners will refuse to budge at all.

Copper and brass

Old copper and brassware has now become quite rare and consequently expensive. The largest grouping of shops selling the old pots, dishes and lamps is in the Christian Quarter of Old Damascus and Old Aleppo.

Jewellery

The bigger cities have their gold souks, especially Damascus and Aleppo, where excellent-value silver jewellery is also to be found, often with semi-precious stones like lapis lazuli, turquoise, coral, jade, black onyx and agate. These come in earrings, necklaces and bracelets and make perfect, easy-to-pack gifts. In

Damascus, silver shops are also located in the Craft Souk and round the edge of the Great Umayyad Mosque.

Spices and herbs

Cumin, cardamom, cinnamon, saffron – the list is endless, you can experiment and they make excellent gifts that add little weight or bulk to your luggage.

Traditional clothing

A number of shops in the souks of Damascus and Aleppo sell both men's and women's old gowns in embroidered silk which make excellent dressing gowns, or even fancy jackets which can be worn to special occasions. The older ones can be quite expensive because of their rarity.

Wooden inlay

Wooden marquetry pieces often inlaid with mother-of-pearl are very popular, the work of the great Damascene cabinetmakers. Their products range from tiny boxes which make novel small gifts, to chess and backgammon sets, Ottoman-style chests and mirrors, even chairs and wardrobes. Straight Street in Damascus has the biggest concentration of these, at the Christian end.

Traditional clothing can be found in the souks

Children

Like all Arabs, Syrians adore children. Each child is special and is regarded as a blessing. The average family size used to be six or seven children, but now, with changing economics, it is tending to shrink to two or three. Whereas the extended family of uncles, aunts and grandparents used to make childcare arrangements easy, the increasing social breakdown of families into smaller units has made the logistics of large families a near impossibility, making each child born all the more precious.

The best age for children visiting Syria is from 8 to 18, when they are old enough to cope with the walking and clambering round the ruins and to remember the experience. Toddlers are tricky and the terrain is not suitable for pushchairs. Babies are no problem as long as you come equipped with high-factor sun cream and have a carrying harness. Pharmacies are recognisable by their green cross, and are very well stocked with the usual range of medicines as well as baby foods, baby creams and nappies, though the latter may not be up to Western standards.

NO SPECIAL TREATMENT

Syria offers almost nothing specifically for children. There are no theme parks, no kiddies' menus, no playgrounds. Children play in the street kicking empty cans round and seem genuinely happy. They are generally not pressurised by pushy parents or teachers, so they can just get on with the business of being children and messing about enjoying their childhood. Electronic gadgets are still a rarity and very few have their own mobile phone or their own computer. Both parents enjoy huge respect, and the father's word on all matters is final.

Beaches

The Mediterranean beaches south of Tartous and north of Lattakia in Syria's Côte d'Azur have fine sandy beaches, perfect for children to play on, and the sea is good for swimming with shallow waters and no nasty creatures with stings to watch out for.

Eating out

Syrian restaurants do not go in for special kiddies' food or kiddies' portions. Children are just expected to eat whatever their parents are eating but in smaller quantity. Obesity among children is pretty much unheard of, as there is no junk food.

Hammams

Children love visiting the hammam, and boys under the age of eight are allowed to go with their mothers into the women's hammams. Splashing about with all that water is great fun and no one will tell you off for spilling it on the floor.

Mosques

Parks and playgrounds are something of a rarity in Syria, but in practice, children treat wherever they happen to be as a playground. The huge open courtyard of the Great Umayyad Mosque, for example, is a wonderful place for chase and hide-and-seek behind the pillars, and the adults can enjoy a peaceful time while the children run happily and safely round.

Ruins

Syria's Roman ruins, such as Palmyra, Apamea and Bosra, are like huge outdoor adventure playgrounds for children. The Dead Cities are also great fun for hiding in and among the ancient houses, while the Crusader castles with their dungeons and towers are sure to fire the imagination of most youngsters.

Mothers come to the mosque for a peaceful chat while their older children run around

Essentials

Arriving and departing

By air

Syria has two international airports, Damascus and Aleppo. The majority of visitors arrive at Damascus, a small airport by international standards. The money-changing booth before you go through passport control is a very convenient place to get Syrian currency, and the rate is good. In the arrivals hall you'll find car hire offices, tour operators and the newly compulsory taxi desk. You will need to have SYP600 on you for the taxi fare into the centre, a journey of 30 minutes (30km/ 19 miles) in normal conditions.

On departure make sure you have SYP200 on you for the airport departure tax (to be purchased after check-in), and SYP75 for the baggage trolley if you need one. The taxi fare out to the airport from the city centre costs SYP500. Check-in is two hours before take-off. The departures hall is surprisingly comfortable, bright and airy, with good souvenir and chocolate shops as well as duty free areas.

The national carrier is **Syrian Arab Airlines** (*27 Albemarle Street, London W1X 3HF. Tel: (020) 7493 2851. www.syriaair.com*). It offers the cheapest flights from European capitals and is the only airline to fly direct to Damascus from London and other European cities. Bookings can be made by phone and are held without deposit until 14 days before travel. Return flights must be reconfirmed at the Syrian end at least 72 hours before the flight.

From London the other major carrier to Syria is **BMI** (*www.flybmi.com*), along with **Air France** (*www.airfrance.com*) and **KLM** (*www.klm.com*), but all involve a stopover either at Beirut, or in Paris or Amsterdam. Check prices on the following: *www.expedia.co.uk*, *www.lastminute.com* and *www.travelocity.com*

By land

You can drive your own car into Syria from Turkey, Lebanon or Jordan, buying a temporary customs waiver at the border costing about US$50, along with third party insurance at about US$40 a month. Procedures are slow at the borders, with many separate stages, and you should always allow at least an hour.

Long-distance deluxe buses are an efficient and extremely cheap way to arrive from Turkey, Lebanon or Jordan. The one-way fare from Amman to Damascus, for example, is SYP300. Make sure you have your visa into Syria arranged in advance as it cannot be purchased at the border. Visas into Jordan, Lebanon and Turkey when exiting Syria can all be bought at the border crossings.

By rail

From Istanbul's Haydarpasha Station, Turkish Railways' Toros Express departs on Sunday mornings and arrives at Aleppo 35 hours later. Fares are cheap. Consult *www.seat61.com* for a description of the train.

Customs

Foreign currency worth up to US$5,000 can be brought into the country, and up to SYP2,000 can be taken out. Import/export limits are 200 cigarettes and two bottles of wine/spirits. No meat products, vegetable or olive oils can be taken out of the country.

Refreshment for passers-by in the souk

Electricity

Plugs and sockets are the Continental two-pin type, so take an adapter if travelling with UK mobile chargers, etc. Power supply is 220V, 50Hz. Power cuts occur in the summer in hot weather when the grid is overloaded with A/Cs.

Internet

Internet usage is growing ferociously at about 45 per cent a year. Increasing numbers of hotels have wireless internet connections for laptops in hotel rooms, big hotels have business centres where you can use their computers, and there are cheap internet cafés all over the cities. Outside Damascus and Aleppo, it is more difficult to find easy access.

Maps

The best is the 'Reise Know How 1:600,000' which covers Syria and Lebanon, available at Stanfords in London. In the country the tourist maps available are generally poor.

Money

The Syrian pound is variously abbreviated as SYP, SY, SL or S£, and is pegged to a basket of currencies including the dollar and the euro. Notes come in SYP1,000, 500, 200, 100 and 50 denominations. The small notes are useful for entry fees and taxis. Coins come in SYP25, 10, 5 and 2 and are handy for small tips for doorkeepers, etc.

Changing money

Avoid traveller's cheques as they are cumbersome to change and are only accepted at a limited number of banks. Cash in sterling, dollars or euros is best. Big hotels have money-changing facilities, but the rate will be better in a bank. It is best to change as much as you think you will need at the airport kiosk on arrival. There are also several ATMs in Damascus and in Aleppo which dispense up to a daily limit of £200-worth. They seem to work efficiently.

Credit and debit cards

Plastic is increasingly accepted in hotels, and in the upmarket restaurants and in the better souvenir shops. VISA and MasterCard are the best and most widely accepted.

Opening hours

All banks, souks and most offices close on Friday, though in Christian areas the shops close on Sunday. Government offices and embassies are open 8am–3pm, banks 8am–6pm, shops generally 9am–2pm & 4–7pm, souks

Typical Damascus tilework

10am–10pm, and museums and sites 9am–6pm (summer), 9am–4pm (winter), closed Tuesdays. In Ramadan hours are foreshortened and most places will close at 3pm.

Passports and visas

Visas must be obtained from the Syrian embassy in your home country before you leave. In London visas take 4–5 days to process and are valid for a 15-day stay, extendable on arrival at the Ministry of the Interior. Single-entry visas are valid for three months and multiple-entry visas are valid for six. Your passport must contain no Israeli stamp. Visa application forms can be downloaded from the Syrian embassy website (*www.syrianembassy.co.uk*) and must be completed in duplicate with two passport photos and a letter of 'sponsorship'. This can be anything on headed paper confirming your identity and your travel to Syria as a tourist.

Pharmacies

All big cities have a rotating 24-hour pharmacy. Only Damascus has a fixed 24-hour one (*Tel: (011) 445 2074*). Pharmacies are well provisioned and most pharmacists speak some English.

Post

Stamps are sold by bookshops, newsagents, and some souvenir shops and hotel receptions. Postcards back to Europe take around three weeks. Post boxes are yellow and scattered about the cities. Avoid leaving items for hotel receptions to post, as this is often unreliable.

Public holidays

On top of the religious holidays (*see pp20–21*), standard secular public holidays are as follows:

New Year	1 January
Revolution Day	8 March
Mothers' Day	21 March
Evacuation Day	17 April (evacuation of the French in 1946, national day)
Labour Day	1 May
Martyrs' Day	6 May
Christmas day	25 December

Smoking

Smoking is permitted pretty much everywhere except in the airport departures and arrivals halls and on board flights. There are no non-smoking restaurants or bars.

Suggested reading and media

Books

Burns, Ross, *Monuments of Syria*, IB Tauris, 1999. Excellent reference work on the archaeology and architecture by a former Australian ambassador.

Christie, Agatha, *Come Tell Me How You Live*, HarperCollins, 1999. Entertaining read about her time accompanying husband archaeologist Max Mallowan on digs in Syria.

Dalrymple, William, *From the Holy Mountain: A Journey in the shadow of Byzantium*, Flamingo, 1998. Following in the footsteps of two monks from Mt Athos in Greece, through Turkey, Syria, Palestine and Egypt, examining the remnants of Eastern Christianity.

Keenan, Brigid, *Hidden Treasures of the Old City*, Thames and Hudson, 2001. Beautifully photographed coffee-table book, a well-researched and sensitive tribute to the heritage of the Old City of Damascus.

Lovell, Mary S, *A Scandalous Life: The Biography of Jane Digby*, Fourth Estate, 1995. Fascinating account of the ups and downs of this English aristocrat.

Glain, Stephen, *Dreaming of Damascus: Merchants, Mullahs and Militants in the Near Middle East*, John Murray, 2003. Poignant account of how the Arab world may collapse without the necessary reform, with militant Islam coming to fill the vacuum.

Hourani, Albert, *A History of the Arabs*, Faber/Warner, 1992. Highly regarded study of the social and political history of the Arabs.

Maalouf, Amin, *The Crusades through Arab Eyes*, Al-Saqi Books, 1984. Refreshingly original insights into the forces that have shaped the Arab consciousness today.

Seale, Patrick, *The Struggle for the Middle East*, IB Tauris, 1988. Based on many personal interviews with the Assad family, well written and scholarly.

Newspapers

The only English daily is the *Syria Times*, an uninspiring compilation of authorised articles, but useful for listings of cultural events, emergency numbers and exchange rates.

TV and radio

The big hotels all have satellite TV and offer BBC World and CNN. BBC World Service can be found on medium wave frequencies, as can Voice of America. Most Syrians tune in to Al-Jazeera, the Qatar-based independent TV channel, for their news coverage. There are two Syrian TV channels, whose programmes are listed in the *Syria Times*. Their staples are Egyptian films, sitcoms and soaps.

Telephones

Most adults have a mobile in Syria and coverage is excellent, even in the middle of the desert. There are competing GSM networks, and UK mobiles work well, though Blackberries don't, since they need a GPRS network. Texting is the cheapest way to keep in touch with family and friends in the UK, and if you want to be able to speak locally on your mobile, you can buy a Syrian SIM card for just SYP400 and then buy pay-as-you-go credit starting from SYP300 a week.

Time differences

Syria is usually two hours ahead of the UK, except in October as clocks go back at the end of September, when it is only one hour ahead. Clocks go forward at the end of March, the same as the UK, so it stays in synchronisation at two hours ahead. Comparative times in other countries for most of the year are as follows:

Australia 7 hours ahead
Canada 7 hours behind
New Zealand 10 hours ahead
South Africa same
United Kingdom 2 hours behind
United States (east coast) 7 hours behind

Toilets

There are almost no public toilets in Syria, but in towns and cities you can use facilities in hotels, restaurants and museums without charge. Usually there is a mixture of squat-type toilets and Western-style sitting toilets. Often there is no toilet paper but a hose is provided for washing instead.

Travellers with disabilities

Syria has virtually no facilities for travellers with disabilities, and exploring any of the cities or sites by wheelchair would present a major challenge because of the uneven surfaces.

A traditional shop in the craft souk in Damascus

Language

Arabic, along with Hebrew, is a Semitic language, completely unrelated grammatically to Indo-European languages like English, French and German. All words in Arabic are based on three-consonant roots from which meanings are then developed. The root *ktb*, for example, conveys the idea of writing, so *maktab* means place of writing or office, *kaataba* is a verb meaning to correspond and *maktoub* means a letter or thing that has been written.

The Arabic alphabet has 29 consonants and three vowels, and all letters are written differently according to their position in the word, which is why the script seems so complicated. In practice, the script is the simplest thing about Arabic, as it obeys set rules and can be memorised in a matter of days. English is the most widely spoken foreign language in Syria, but whilst you can get by without Arabic, it is always appreciated if you know a few words. The older generation speaks French, but this is dying out, as are they.

Greetings

Hello	**Marhaba**
Welcome	**Ahlan wa-sahlan**
Goodbye	**Ma'a as-salaama**
Formal greeting (by person arriving)	**As-salaamu 'alaykum** (Peace be upon you)
Reply to greeting (by person in situ)	**Wa 'alaykum as salaam**

Basics

Yes	**Aiwa, na'am**
No	**Laa**
Please	**Min fadlak**
Thank you	**Shukran**
Thank you very much	**Shukran jazeelan**
Sorry, excuse me	**Muta'assif**
Hurry up, let's go	**Yallah**
Good	**Kwayyis, tayyib**
Bad	**Mish kwayyis**
A lot, very	**Kateer**
Very good	**Kwayyis kateer**
No problem	**Mish mishkila**
Never mind	**Ma'a laysh**
Bank	**Bank, masraf**
Post office	**Maktab bareed**
Museum	**Mathaf**

Directions

Right	**Yameen**
Left	**Yasaar**
Straight on	**Dhughri**

How far is it to...?	**Kam kilometre ila...?**
Where is...?	**Wayn...?**

Restaurants

The bill	**Al-faatoura**
Breakfast	**Futour**
Lunch	**Ghada**
Dinner	**'Ashaa**
Without meat	**Bi-doon lahm**
Tea	**Shay**
Coffee	**'Ahwa**
Sugar	**Sukkar**
Wine	**Nabeedh**
Red wine	**Nabeedh ahmar**
White wine	**Nabeedh abyad**
Beer	**Beera**
Cold	**Baared**
Bread	**Khubz**
Water	**Mai**
Butter	**Zibdeh**
Jam	**Murabbeh**
Honey	**'Asl**
Milk	**Haleeb**
Eggs	**Bayd**
Cheese	**Jibneh**
Vegetables	**Khudar**
Yogurt	**Laban**

Shopping

Half kilo	**Nuss kilo**
Cheap	**Rakhees**
Expensive	**Ghaali**
How much?	**Bikaam?**

Time

Today	**Al-yawm**
Tomorrow	**Bukra**
Yesterday	**Ams**
Monday	**Yawm al-ithnayn**
Tuesday	**Yawm ath-thalaatha**
Wednesday	**Yawm al-arba'a**
Thursday	**Yawm al-khamees**
Friday	**Yawm al-jum'a**
Saturday	**Yawm as-sabt**
Sunday	**Yawm al-ahad**
Early	**Bakkeer**
Late	**Muta'akhir**

Numbers

1	**Waahad**
2	**Ithnayn**
3	**Thalaatha**
4	**Arba'a**
5	**Khamsa**
6	**Sitta**
7	**Sab'a**
8	**Thamaania**
9	**Tis'a**
10	**'Ashara**
20	**'Ashreen**
30	**Thalaatheen**
40	**Arba'een**
50	**Khamseen**
60	**Siteen**
70	**Sab'een**
80	**Thamaaneen**
90	**Tis'een**
100	**Mi'a**
150	**Mi'a wa khamseen**
200	**Mi'atayn**
500	**Khams mi'a**
1,000	**Alf**
2,000	**Alfayn**

Emergencies

Emergency numbers

Ambulance *110*
Fire *113*
Police *112*

Medical services

Doctors, dentists and opticians are all well trained, competent and English-speaking. For minor ailments consult a pharmacist who will also be well qualified. You are always recommended to take out comprehensive medical insurance before travel.

The following recommended private hospitals in Damascus are well known to taxi drivers:

Al-Chami Hospital (takes VISA, MasterCard, American Express) *Tel: (011) 373 4925.*
French Hospital *Tel: (011) 444 0460.*
Italian Hospital *Tel: (011) 332 6030.*
24-hour central pharmacy *Tel: (011) 445 2074.*

Health risks

The strong sun is probably the biggest health risk, so come equipped with high-factor sun cream (not readily available in the country, and expensive when it is). Wear a hat and avoid walking round ruins between 11am and 3pm. Carry a bottle of mineral water round with you.

Holiday diarrhoea is the next most likely problem, a reaction to the oiliness of food rather than specific bacteria. Buy a packet of Ercifuryl capsules from the pharmacy which will sort out any stomach problems, or bring Imodium with you.

Strong winds and dust can give sensitive eyes problems, for which pharmacists sell drops.

Police

The only police you are likely to encounter are the traffic police who stand at junctions directing traffic. Otherwise they are not in evidence. Police checkpoints in the country are near sensitive border areas such as the Golan and near Mari close to the Iraqi border.

Safety and crime

Syria, contrary to its popularly portrayed image in the Western media, is one of the safest countries in the world. There is no violent or petty crime to speak of, such acts being seen as degrading and bringing shame and dishonour to your family. Theft and pickpocketing are rare for the same reason, and are more likely to be perpetrated by other foreigners, especially visiting Russians renewing their visas. However, it is wise to take the usual precautions in the souks, making sure your money and passport are out of sight. Walking alone at night in the streets of Damascus as a woman presents no problems.

The concept of 'health and safety' is still in its infancy in Syria, and you will notice how, compared to Western obsessions, there is little attempt to put up safety railings on vertiginous edges at Crusader castles, for example, let alone to wear helmets on bikes or motorbikes. Extended families of 20 upwards can be seen crowded into the back of an open pick-up truck, or up to seven people squashed onto one moped. Rear seat belts are something of a rarity, and using front ones is far from automatic. Such matters are entrusted to God.

Embassies

All embassies are closed Friday and Saturday, and open 8am–3.15pm other days.

Australian Embassy Australian nationals are looked after by the Canadian Embassy (*see below*).

British Embassy *Kurd Ali St, Kotob Building, Malki PO Box 37. Tel: (011) 373 9241.*

Canadian Embassy *Lot 12, Autostrade Mezzeh PO Box 3394. Tel: (011) 611 6692.*

New Zealand The closest consulate is in Amman, Jordan (*tel: (962) 6 463 6720*), and the closest embassy is in Ankara, Turkey (*tel: (90) 312 467 9054*).

South African Embassy *7 Jadet Kouraish, Al-Ghazaoui St, West Mezzeh PO Box 9141. Tel: (011) 613 51520. Email: saembdam@scs-net.org*

United States Embassy *2 Al-Mansour St, Abu Roumaneh PO Box 29. Tel: (011) 333 3052.*

The sun can be dangerously strong in Syria

Directory

Accommodation price guide

Accommodation prices are based on an average double room for two people sharing, including breakfast and taxes. Most hotels still price in US dollars, though some are starting to use euros.

★	Under US$25
★★	US$25–75
★★★	US$75–175
★★★★	Over US$175

Eating out price guide

Prices are based on the average cost of a meal for two without alcohol. With beer or *'araq*, add 50 per cent to the bill, with a bottle of wine, add 100 per cent.

★	Under US$10
★★	US$10–20
★★★	US$20–40
★★★★	Over US$40

DAMASCUS AND AROUND

Damascus

ACCOMMODATION

Al-Haramain ★
A popular, rambling 19th-century Ottoman house round a covered courtyard, partially renovated, with a range of rooms. Its clientele are mainly students and backpackers looking for the cheapest place to stay, and certainly no Syrians stay here. Located a five-minute walk away from the Old City, tucked up a quiet side street in the Souk Sarouja area. Offers breakfast but no other meals. 15 rooms.
Bahsa St, Sarouja. Tel: (011) 231 9489. Email: alharamain_hotel@yahoo.com

Al-Rabie ★
Tucked up the same side street as Al-Haramain, but with a larger courtyard and bar area, Al-Rabie now offers five rooms with simple WC/shower ensuite for a slightly higher price. Breakfast in the spacious courtyard. Similar clientele to Al-Haramain. 15 rooms.
Bahsa St, Sarouja. Tel: (011) 231 8374. Email: alrabiehotel@hotmail.com

Al-Saada ★
Just 100m (110yds) further into the Sarouja district from Al-Rabie and Al-Haramain, this simple but attractive place is also in a converted 19th-century house. Breakfast is offered in the courtyard. 12 rooms.
Sarouja. Tel: (011) 231 1722. Fax: (011) 231 1875.

Sultan ★★
Very close to the Hejaz Railway station, just five minutes' walk from the Old City, this is an excellent budget choice. Rooms are simple but clean, some have A/C. Breakfast, but no other meals. Friendly staff. Favoured by archaeologists en route to digs.
Al-Baroudi St. Tel: (011) 222 5768. Email: sultan.hotel@mail.sy

Al-Majed ★★★
In a quiet location up a small street close to the Cham Palace Hotel, this establishment has a sister hotel next door, Al-Khayyam. The rooms are small and simple but equipped with huge fridges, reflecting their mainly Arab clientele's propensity to eat copiously in their rooms. There is a rooftop restaurant, and outdoor seating areas in the driveway. 100 rooms.
Just off 29 May Street. Tel: (011) 232 3300. Email: majed@almajed-group.com. www.almajed-group.com

Omayad ★★★
An excellent-value hotel in the middle category, unusual in Damascus, much used by businessmen and small groups. Well run by a Lebanese manager, it belongs to the Swiss International Hotels group, and all rooms are spacious and have wireless internet connections. Buffet-style breakfast is served in the small bar area. The rooftop restaurant is only used for functions, but the room service menu is excellent. It is well located in a quiet street close to the Cham Palace Hotel and the Avicenne bookshop, just five minutes' walk from the National Museum and 20 minutes' walk from the Old City. Reservations can be made online. 80 rooms.
Brazil St, PO Box 7811. Tel: (011) 221 7700. Email: omayad-hotel@net.sy. www.omayad-hotel.com

Venezia ★★★
Recently renovated and popular with tour groups from Spain and Sweden, this mid-range hotel has adequate if unexciting rooms, and one restaurant. 75 rooms. Located on a main road near the French Cultural Institute between the Cham Palace Hotel and the Old City, ten minutes' walk away.
Youssef Al-Azmah St. Tel: (011) 231 6631. Email: info@venezia-syria.com. www.venezia-syria.com

Beit Al-Mamlouka ★★★★
With just eight exquisite rooms set round the courtyard of an 18th/19th-century house, this bijou boutique hotel was the first to open within the walls, in April 2005. The restoration project took three years and each room is totally different, from the stunning Suleyman the Magnificent suite with its painted ceiling, to the slightly more modest Haroun Ar-Rashid. There are roof terraces where you can sit and read, and breakfast is taken in the high-ceilinged bar area. Other meals can be taken by prior arrangement. Located in the Christian Quarter close to the Elissar restaurant and opposite the Hammam Bakri. Taxi service to and from the airport.
Bab Touma, PO Box 34049. Tel: (011) 543 0445. Email: almamlouka@mail.sy. www.almamlouka.com

Cham Palace Hotel ★★★★
For many years the premier hotel in the country, now eclipsed by the Four Seasons, this is the headquarters of the Cham Palace Hotel group, which has

branches in Aleppo, Palmyra, Deir Ez-Zour, Bosra, Safita and Hama. It is very well located in the heart of the commercial district, 1.5km (1 mile) from the Old City, and its tall circular tower topped by the gold revolving restaurant, L'Etoile d'Or, is something of a landmark. The car hire office Chamcar, affiliated with Hertz, is next door. The grand lobby with its cavernous ceiling height is worth having a drink in, even if you're not staying. Upstairs there is an indoor pool, fitness centre and beauty salon. There are five restaurants, 24-hour money changing and a small bookshop off the lobby. 400 rooms.
Maisaloun St, PO Box 7570. Tel: (011) 223 2300. Email: chamresa@net.sy. www.chamhotels.com

Ebla Cham ★★★★
This enormous luxury pile is out near the airport and is much frequented by businessmen and conference-goers. Its sports facilities are some of the best in the country, boasting the only 18-hole golf course in Syria. It also has a pool, 4 tennis courts and a fitness centre.
440 rooms.
PO Box 6416. Tel: (011) 224 1900. Email: chamebla@net.sy. www.chamhotels.com

Four Seasons ★★★★
The newest addition to Damascus' top-end luxury hotels, this unmistakable 23-storey hulk in white with green glass (reminiscent of the MI6 building in London) opened in late 2005. Extremely well situated overlooking the trickle of the Barada River and close to the National Museum, it is about 2km (1¼ miles) from the Old City. It was built with Saudi money in what used to be a park, and boasts all the usual 5-star facilities including a surprisingly small pool, health club and business centre. There are five restaurants and a nightclub. 381 rooms.
Shukri Al-Quwatly St. Tel: (011) 339 1000. Email: reservations.dam@fourseasons.com. www.fourseasons-syria.com

Meridien ★★★★
Further out of town near Umawiyeen Square and about 0.5km (1/3 mile) from the National Museum, this was the first luxury hotel to be built in Damascus, back in the 1970s. Set in its own greenery, it offers a pool, tennis courts, a business centre and a shopping mall, with a car hire agency linked to Europcar. It has five restaurants and 350 rooms.
Shukri Al-Quwatly St. Tel: (011) 373 8730. www.lemeridien.com

Semiramis ★★★★
The cheapest of the 5-star hotels, the Semiramis is very centrally located on a busy square just five minutes' walk from the Old City. It has a small rooftop pool (indoor and outdoor) and a health centre, along with a car hire agency linked to Europcar. Of its four restaurants, one is Chinese, and its nightclub has live singers.

115 rooms.
Victoria Bridge, PO Box 30301. Tel: (011) 223 3555. Email: semiramis@net.sy. www.semiramis-hotel.com

Sheraton ★★★★
Trickily located west of Umawiyeen Square beside a maze of roads, a 15-minute taxi ride from the commercial centre and the Old City, the hotel is used mainly by businessmen or wealthy Gulf Arabs. It enjoys all the usual 5-star facilities. 278 rooms.
Umawiyeen Square, PO Box 4795. Tel: (011) 373 4639. Email: resv_sheraton@net.sy. www.starwood.com

Talisman ★★★★
A wonderful fantasy of a place arranged round two courtyards yet with just 16 rooms, the Talisman is discreetly tucked away in the Old City's Jewish Quarter, 100m (110yds) south of the Roman Arch on Straight Street. It opened in March 2006 and the main courtyard has an enormous 1.8m (6ft) deep pool, the only swimming pool in the Old City. Originally an 18th-century ruin, it has benefited from extensive reconstruction. All rooms are traditionally furnished, with central heating, air conditioning and plasma TV screens, DVD player and internet connection. It even has its own private Turkish bath. There are magnificent reception lounges for reading or coffee, and light meals are served in the restaurant. Excellent value at the bottom end of the top price band.
116 Tal El-Hijara St. Tel: (011) 541 5379. Email: reservation@ hoteltalisman.net. www.hoteltalisman.net

Eating out

Abou Al-Izz ★★
Just off the Souk Al-Hamadiye at the Great Umayyad Mosque end, up an unlikely looking staircase, this rambling place is spread over several levels, and is much frequented by locals and other Arab nationalities. No alcohol, but portions are huge, offering the usual Arab fare of *mezze* and kebabs.

Bait Jabri ★★
Tricky to find the first time, tucked down a back-street between the Umayyad Mosque and Straight Street, this beautiful palace was the first converted restaurant to open in the Old City. The courtyard seating is very popular and often quite full, with a good mix of locals and foreigners. No alcohol, but one of the few restaurants to serve falafel at lunch time.
Zukak Al-Sawwaf. Tel: (011) 541 6254. Email: jabrihouse@yahoo.com. www.jabrihouse.com

Barjees ★★
Right in the southern part of the Muslim Quarter near Bab Al-Saghir, this huge cavernous place is an alcohol-free converted courtyard house offering good Arabic cuisine. In a room off the restaurant it has a private cinema where it occasionally shows films to small audiences.
Bab Al-Saghir.

Haretna ★★
Attractive, good-value place in the Christian Quarter with street seating. There are good fruit cocktails here, but no alcohol.
Bab Touma, near Ousrat Al-Ikhaa Al-Sourieh. Tel: (011) 544 1184.

Leila's ★★
In a stunning location directly next to the Great Umayyad Mosque, with a roof terrace right under the Jesus Minaret. Occasional alcohol (beer is discreetly served and sometimes wine if you are lucky), and a good-value range of *mezze* and kebabs.
Southeast corner of the Umayyad Mosque. Tel: (011) 544 5900.

Narcissus Palace ★★
In the heart of the Muslim Quarter this converted courtyard restaurant offers Arabic food but no alcohol. It has an incongruous flat TV screen embedded into its rear old wall, and is popular with young Syrian women smoking *narghils.*
Tel: (011) 541 6785.

Al-Dar ★★★
Unusual venue in the Christian Quarter, architect-built from scratch but in the old style with a lot of black basalt. Arabic cuisine of a high standard and good wine and *'araq* on offer.
Beside Assieh School. Tel: (011) 542 3232.

Al-Khawali ★★★
Located just off Straight Street near Bait Siba'i tucked down an unlikely alley with a very discreet entrance, Al-Khawali is an enormous converted Ottoman palace, traditionally furnished on two levels plus an extensive roof terrace with superb views over the domes of Khan As'ad Pasha, Damascus' grandest caravanserai, towards Jebel Qassioun. It does not serve alcohol but to compensate does excellent juices and bakes its own fresh Arabic bread to order. Arabic cuisine with a superb variety of *mezze.*
Off Straight St. Tel: (011) 222 5808.

Arabesque ★★★
In the heart of the Christian Quarter within the walls of the Old City, this European-style restaurant offers excellent French/Italian cuisine in a very gentle and sophisticated setting. Pleasant roof terrace with attractive foliage and views to Jebel Qassioun. Good wine list.
Sharia Al-Kineesa. Tel: (011) 541 4638.

Casablanca ★★★
Near Bab Sharqi on the eastern edge of the Christian Quarter, this plush place is in a converted Ottoman house and offers chic French cuisine at rather inflated prices. Good wine list, and live music after 10.30pm.
Hanania St, Bab Sharqi. Tel: (011) 541 9000.

Elissar ★★★
The name Elissar is the Phoenician version of Dido, Queen of Carthage. This was one of the first restaurants to open in a converted 19th-century courtyard house. The space is huge and there are extensive roof terraces as well. Arabic cuisine with alcohol served. Close to

Bab Touma in the Christian Quarter and very close to Bait Al-Mamlouka and Hammam Bakri.
Sharia Ad-Dawamneh, Bab Touma. Tel: (011) 542 4300.

La Montagna ★★★
Located up on Jebel Qassioun, this place has dramatic views from its terraces over the city below, especially fine at night. The menu is Italian and international, with a good selection of pasta and pizza. No alcohol but good juices.
Jebel Qassioun. Tel: (011) 373 1110.

Oriental ★★★
Tucked down a side street near the Greek Catholic Patriarchate just off Straight Street, this place offers excellent Arabic cuisine with delicacies like fresh artichokes. Set in a restored courtyard house, there is a live *'oud* (lute) player in the evenings.
Zeitouna St. Tel: (011) 543 1324.

Etoile D'Or ★★★★
This classy establishment is Damascus' only revolving restaurant, located on the top floor of the Cham Palace Hotel. A complete revolution takes two hours, and the setting is superb, with excellent Arabic food and good service, as well as a good wine list. An experience not to be rushed.
Cham Palace Hotel, Maisaloun St. Tel: (011) 223 2300.

Entertainment

Bars, cafés and clubs

Albal Café and Gallery
Lovely café with a young, bohemian feel; easy to visit as a lone female.
Shaweesh St, Old City. Tel: (011) 544 5794.

Four Seasons Nightclub
The most expensive venue in town, overpriced and sophisticated. Live music.
Four Seasons Hotel. Tel: (011) 339 1000. Open: from 10.30pm.

Marmar
A younger venue with a late-night dance bar and music that ranges from classical in the week to the latest hits at the weekend.
Al-Dawamneh St, Old City. Tel: (011) 544 6425.

Meridien Nightclub
Expensive and a bit soulless and bland.
Meridien Hotel. Tel: (011) 373 8730. Open: from 10.30pm.

Nawfara Café
Behind the Umayyad Mosque, a storyteller (*hakawaati*) goes into action most evenings from around 7pm, the only one left. Fascinating as an experience, even if you do not understand a word, to hear the rhetorical power of the Arabic language.
Nawfara St. Open: 10am–10pm.

Oxygen
In the Christian Quarter, well signposted, is this stylish bar with food. Relatively expensive, it attracts a more grown-up clientele.
Off Bab Touma St. Tel: (011) 544 4398.

Piano Bar
In the Christian Quarter near Bab Sharqi, live music and restaurant.
Hanania St, Bab Sharqi. Open: 10.30pm–2am.

Semiramis Nightclub
Live singers.
Semiramis Hotel, Victoria Bridge. Tel: (011) 223

3555. Open: from 10.30pm.

Straight Street
Half way along the street, beyond the Roman Arch in the Christian Quarter, the only out-and-out bar in the Old City, frequented almost entirely by men.
Open: evenings only.

Umayyad Palace
Down an alley just by the Great Umayyad Mosque, this over-the-top basement restaurant is the one place where you can watch Whirling Dervishes perform (from 9pm). The show sometimes includes acrobats and musicians.
Sharia Al-Masbagha Al-Khader.
Tel: (011) 222 0826.
Open: noon–2am.

Cinema

Cham Cinema
Attached to the Cham Palace Hotel (*see pp161–2*), this is the best place for Western films. Two screens, one in English. Cheap tickets. Listings published in *Syria Times.*
Maisaloun St.

Culture

British Council
Occasional cultural performances by visiting British artists.
Maisaloun St, Saalan. Tel: (011) 331 0631. Email: general.inquiries@bc/damascus.bcouncil.org

Dar Al-Assad
The modern opera house near Umawiyeen Square, used by the National Symphony orchestra for its performances and for visiting artists. Listings in the *Syria Times.*
Tel: (011) 224 3508.
www.opera-syria.org

French Cultural Centre
The most active of the cultural centres, offering French language and computer courses, and organising cultural performances of plays, concerts and exhibitions with French artists.
Bahsa St. Tel: (011) 231 6181. www.ccf-damas.org

Goethe Institute
Provides German language tuition and cultural events put on by visiting German performers.
60 Adnan Malki St, PO Box 6100. Tel: (011) 333 6673. www.goethe.de/ins/sy/dam.org

Hammams

Al-Malik Az-Zaher
Close to the Zahiriye Madrasa where Baibars the great Mameluke Sultan is buried, this hammam takes its name too from the epithet of Baibars, 'zaher' meaing radiant, glorious. Its changing room is very fine, but the inner hot and steam rooms are less exciting. Men only except Mondays when women are given free rein all day.
Zahiriye St.
Tel: (011) 222 4975.

Hammam Bakri
Opposite Bait Al-Mamlouka in Bab Touma, this later and more simple hammam is for women from 10am–4pm, then men from 5–10pm daily.
Qanayet Al-Hatab St.
Tel: (011) 542 6606.

Hammam Silsila
Also known as the Roman Baths, these baths are open 9am–11pm, offering the full range of steam and massage.
Old City.
Tel: (011) 222 0279.

Nur Ed-Din
This is the finest and oldest hammam in

Damascus, with magnificent 12th-century marble chambers, and it offers the full range of sauna, steam room and massage. Men only. The admission price includes a massage. Tea and snacks are available.
Al-Bezouriye St in the Spice Market, Old City.
Tel: (011) 222 9513.

Galleries

Art House
A gallery for exhibiting modern Syrian artists such as the sculptor Mustafa Ali. It also hosts concerts featuring local classical musicians like Lebanese violinist Jihad Akel and the Syrian jazz band Ertijal.
In Mezzeh, behind the children's hospital.
Tel: (011) 333 3924.

Ayyam Gallery
An art gallery exhibiting leading Syrian artists such as Louay Kayyali, Adham Ismail and Mahmoud Hammad.
Mezzeh West Villas, 30 Chile St.
Tel: (011) 613 1088.

Spanish Cultural Centre
(Instituto Cervantes)
Regularly shows Spanish films and occasionally hosts concerts by visiting Spanish musicians.
Malek Abdel Aziz Al Saud St. Tel: (011) 373 7061.

Sport and leisure

The 5-star hotels have pools, gyms and tennis courts. Otherwise there is nothing except Al-Andalous, an open-air swimming pool complex in Derreyah, surrounded by attractive cacti, much used in the summer months for cooling off.

Bosra

Accommodation

Bosra Cham Hotel ★★★
The smallest in the Cham Hotel group, with just 50 rooms, this is the only place worth considering if you want a base in the south. Just a few minutes' walk from the Roman Theatre, set in pleasant greenery. Open-air pool May–Oct and a handful of shops.
Tel: (015) 790 881.
www.chamhotels.com

Eating out

Bosra Cham Hotel ★★★
The only place where alcohol is served, with a quiet dining room overlooking the garden and buffet food if you coincide with a group, otherwise à la carte.
Tel: (015) 790 881.
www.chamhotels.com

Maaloula

Accommodation

Maaloula Hotel ★★★
Superb location on the rock overlooking the village below, beside Mar Sarkis Monastery, this is the best by far in the area, with outdoor swimming pool, sauna and tennis court. Hall for banquets and conferences, coffee house, bar, pizza restaurant and terrace restaurant. Monastery caves within the grounds, converted to bars.
37 rooms.
PO Box Maaloula 15.
Tel: (012) 777 0250.
Email: maaloula@scs-net.org

Eating out

Al-Reef Terrace Restaurant ★★
Fabulous location on terraces below the Maaloula Hotel,

serving Arabic and international cuisine. *Tel: (012) 777 0250.*

Family Restaurant ★★
Simple place in the square opposite Mar Thekla Monastery in the town, serving its own thick heavy wine, with basic Syrian food like kebabs, omelette and vegetable starters.

Seydnaya

Accommodation

Seydnaya Hotel ★
Simple place on the western edge of town with a small outdoor pool (late May–mid-Oct) and lovely views over the snow-capped peaks of the Anti-Lebanon range. Very popular with Lebanese pilgrims. Avoid Saturdays as it is always full. 27 rooms. *Tel: (011) 595 0358.*

PALMYRA AND BEYOND

Palmyra

Accommodation

Heliopolis ★★
Good-value hotel in the town of Tadmur but tucked down a quiet side street overlooking the palmery. Five storeys high, with an excellent rooftop restaurant for good (if distant) views of the ruins. 35 rooms. *Tel: (031) 913 921. Email: heliopolis-palmyra@usa.net*

Villa Palmyra ★★
Next best in the town after the Heliopolis, on the main street, with a basement bar and rooftop restaurant overlooking the palmery. 40 rooms. *Tel: (031) 913 600. Fax: (031) 912 554.*

Zenoubie Cham Palace ★★★
The original hotel Zenobia from the French Mandate, in its privileged location immediately beside the ruins of Palmyra, beautifully renovated by the Cham group in summer 2007. Its terrace is the favoured spot for sunset drinks and gazing over the view. Single storey, no pool. 24 rooms. Good restaurant serving alcohol. *PO Box 150. Tel: (031) 591 0107. www.chamhotels.com*

Semiramis ★★★★
Opened 2007, at the approach to Palmyra on the left as you arrive from Damascus/Homs, with 117 rooms overlooking the oasis. Pool and tennis courts. The Nabo bar and Adrian coffee shop serve snacks, and main meals are taken in the Tent restaurant. *Tel: (031) 911 111. Email: semiramis@net.sy. www.semiramis-hotel.com*

Eating out

Heliopolis ★★
On the rooftop floor of the same hotel, good-value Arabic cuisine and efficient service. Alcohol served. *Tel: (031) 913 921.*

Zenoubie Cham ★★★
Within the hotel of the same name, this small, intimate restaurant boasts the best views of the ruins, and you can walk from here straight in to explore them. Alcohol served. Arabic and international cuisine. *Tel: (031) 591 0107.*

Entertainment

Zenoubie Cham Hotel has a Bedouin tent attached that serves Bedouin food and sometimes has live music.

Deir Ez-Zour

ACCOMMODATION

Badia Cham ★★★

A little newer but still cheaper than the Furat Cham (*see listing below*), this good hotel is not on the river but is closer in to the town centre about 1km (2/3 mile) away. Restaurant serving alcohol, coffee shop and snack bar. Pool. 80 rooms.

PO Box 219. Tel: (051) 313 401. Email: chambadia@net.sy. www.chamhotels.com

Furat Cham ★★★

In an excellent, quiet location 5km (3 miles) away from the noise and dust of the town centre and on the banks of the Euphrates, this hotel is the most comfortable base in the area. Large outdoor pool overlooking the river. Drinks and meals are served outdoors on the terrace in the warmer months. Tennis courts. Much used by visiting oil exploration employees. 200 rooms.

PO Box 219. Tel: (051) 313 8000. Email: chamfra@net.sy. www.chamhotels.com

EATING OUT

Four Seasons ★★★

In the Furat Cham Hotel this is the swishest in the area and overlooks the river. Serves alcohol and fresh fish from the Euphrates.

Tel: (051) 313 8000.

ORONTES VALLEY AND CITIES OF THE DEAD

Hama

ACCOMMODATION

Noria ★★

Friendly, well-run place, with spacious rooms, next best after the Apamea Cham (*see listing below*). 43 rooms. Satellite TV and fridge in rooms.

Sharia Shoukri Al-Quwatli, PO Box 970. Tel: (033) 512 414. Email: bader@mail.sy

Apamea Cham ★★★

By far the most comfortable base from which to explore the southern Cities of the Dead, this hotel is right in the centre of Hama, overlooking the Orontes River and a pair of waterwheels. A modern 11-storey construction, it was built in the 1980s on a site where the previous buildings had been razed following the Hama Uprising of 1982. Large outdoor pool, tennis courts, and gardens sloping downhill towards the river. 173 rooms.

PO Box 111. Tel: (033) 525 335. www.chamhotels.com

EATING OUT

Family Club Restaurant ★

Near the Roman Orthodox church in the Christian part of town. Friendly, relaxed place, with alcohol, good Arabic cuisine, and attractive first-floor terrace. Food is often served very late, starting from 9pm. Evenings only.

Le Jardin ★

Excellent-value and superb location right on the river below the Apamea Cham Hotel, looking straight across at the waterwheels and Nur Ed-Din mosque. Beer and spirits are served but no wine. Popular with local people who also enjoy *narghiles*. Can be accessed direct from the hotel via a tunnel under the road from the bottom of the hotel garden.

Homs

Accommodation

Safir Hotel ★★★
The only place Homs can offer that is at this level, and hence it serves as the Mecca for all locals, the venue for socialising and drinking. An ugly, modern, five-storey block, it is located 2km (1¼ miles) out of the centre near the train station, and offers an outdoor pool, tennis courts, a coffee bar, two restaurants and conference facilities. 175 rooms.
Ragheb Al-Jamali St, PO Box 17465. Tel: (031) 412 400. Email: safir@net.sy. www.safirhotels.com

Eating out

Mamma Mia ★★
Good Italian restaurant within the Safir Hotel.

Mersia ★★★
Plush restaurant serving international and Arab cuisine, within the Safir Hotel, overlooking the gardens and pool.

ALEPPO AND THE NORTH

Aleppo

Accommodation

Dar Halabia ★
Just inside the Old City near Bab Antakya, this is a modestly converted, simple 18th-century courtyard house with traditionally furnished rooms. A touch basic, but excellent value and clean. Breakfast only. Deadly quiet at night, as Aleppo's Old City shuts down after dark.
Tel: (021) 224 8497. Email: halabiatour@net.sy. www.halabia-tours.com

Baron Hotel ★★
Famous from its earlier guests such as T E Lawrence and Agatha Christie (who wrote part of *Murder on the Orient Express* here), this early 1900s building used to overlook a marsh where game was shot for dinner. Now a shadow of its former self, it is hemmed in on all sides by modern buildings. The bar still has a fine atmosphere of bygone times, however. 30 rooms, rather basically furnished, most with ensuites.
Baron St, PO Box 130. Tel: (021) 211 0880. Email: hotelbaron@mail.sy

Diwan Rasmi ★★
A converted pair of Ottoman houses in an unusual location about ten minutes' walk north of the citadel. Fine citadel views from the terrace restaurant. 32 rooms of varying sizes. No alcohol is served.
Tel: (021) 331 2222.

Amir Palace ★★★
Modern hotel in a good location close to the National Museum and within easy walking distance (five to ten minutes) of the Old City. Excellent food, pleasant bar, good bookshop. No pool. Sauna. 131 rooms.
Hanano St, PO Box. Tel: (021) 221 4800. Email: amir@net.sy

Beit Wakil ★★★
In the Christian Quarter of Al-Jdaideh, this is the converted residence of a former bishop. 16 rooms

arranged round the courtyard, traditionally furnished. Restaurant in the second courtyard.
Al-Jdaideh. Tel: (021) 221 7169. www.beitwakil.com

Dar Zamaria Martini ★★★
In the Christian Quarter, another classily restored 19th-century palace with 22 rooms, traditionally furnished. Cellar bar and chic restaurant open to the public.
Al-Jdaideh. Tel: (021) 363 6100. Email: razahtl@net.sy

Chahba Cham ★★★★
Colossal 11-storey modern monster 2km (1¼ miles) out of the centre in a business suburb. Large outdoor pool, health club. Two restaurants, two bars, good bookshop. 250 rooms.
Sharia Al-Qudsi, PO Box 992. Tel: (021) 227 0100. Email: chamchah@net.sy. www.chamhotels.com

Mansouriya Palace ★★★★
Exquisite 16th-century palace with nine suites, each furnished in a different theme such as Iznik, with lavish tilework, Hittite with black basalt lions in the bathroom, Byzantine, Ottoman and so on. Library, Turkish bath and jacuzzi. Internet connection in all rooms. Tucked away in the Old City near the Bimaristan Arghoun.
Tel: (00 33) 1 44 18 01 80. Email: benedicte@mansouriya.com. www.mansouriya.com

Eating out

Ahlidar ★★
Just north of the tourist entrance to the Great Mosque, a new restaurant is aspiring to great things. Arabic cuisine.

Kan Zamaan ★★
There is an upper eating area reached by a lift, all in an 18th-century converted house.
Tel: (021) 363 0299.

Yasmeen House ★★
Located just opposite Kan Zamaan, in a pretty 18th-century restored house with outdoor courtyard eating.
Arabic cuisine.
Tel: (021) 222 4462.

Bait Sissi ★★★
Arguably Aleppo's best restaurant, sitting in the heart of the Christian Quarter of Al-Jdaideh. Set in a beautifully restored 18th-century courtyard house, it also has a cellar bar and a piano bar.
Tel: (021) 221 9411. Open: noon–midnight.

Bait Wakil ★★★
The restaurant courtyard of the Bait Wakil hotel, open to the public, serves excellent Arabic cuisine.

Beroea ★★★
Swish, very large new place to the north of the citadel, usually very busy with locals; always a good sign.

Dar Zamaria ★★★
The chic restaurant of the Dar Zamaria Martini hotel, with an exclusive clientele. Arabic cuisine.
Tel: (021) 363 6100.

Entertainment

Bars, cafés and clubs

The only nightclubs are in the big hotels, notably the Chahba Cham and the Amir Palace. Live music is sometimes laid on in the evenings at Bait Wakil and Kan Zamaan.

Ramsis Tea House
Pleasant upmarket café with real expressos, *café*

au lait and tea instead of the usual Turkish/Arabic coffee. Reasonable prices. *Baron St, opposite the Syrian Air office.*

Cinema

The Chahba Cham Hotel has the only cinema showing Western films, reached from its foyer. Cinemas tend to be male-only experiences.

Sport and leisure

Fun Time
An area of bright colourful children's amusements, with slides, tunnels and bouncy ball courts.
Dream Park (approached via Usman Pasha St to the northwest end of the park, north of Quwatly St). Open: daily 10am–10pm.

Game Land
Modern ten-pin bowling alley, also with snooker and billiards tables.
Dream Park. Open: daily 10am–10pm.

Grand Fitness Centre
Best and largest sports complex in Aleppo with an Olympic-size pool and poolside café, fully equipped gym, tennis courts and health club with sauna, jacuzzi and steam room.
University St, next to Pullman Shahba Hotel. Tel: (021) 268 8001. Open: daily 6am–11pm. Women-only sessions: Mon, Wed, Sat 2–6pm & Tue, Thur, Sun 10am–2pm.

THE SYRIAN COAST

Amrit

Accommodation

A 5-star hotel was under construction on the beach near Amrit in 2007.

Krak des Chevaliers

Accommodation

Al-Wadi ★★★
The best-located of the local hotels situated in the valley directly below the castle with fine views up to it. 4km (2½ miles) away from the castle by road. 50 spacious rooms, the best are on the fourth and fifth floors. High ceilings and balconies. Pool, good restaurant.
Tel: (043) 730 456. Fax: (043) 730 399.

Francis ★★★
Large apartment hotel on a hillside some 6km (3¾ miles) from Krak itself. Fine mountain views, but not of the castle. Large pool, bar and terrace. In summer it is packed with holidaying Gulf families. 50 suites.
Tel: (043) 730 946. www.francishotel.net

Eating out

Al-Kala'a ★
In an excellent position overlooking the Krak from above, behind the aqueduct, reached by following the road round the foot of the walls. A simple place offering chicken and *mezze*. Go early or late to miss the coach tours.

Lattakia

Accommodation

Cham Côte D'Azur ★★★
The best of the beach hotels north of Lattakia, with a fine sandy beach, water sports, tennis courts and mini-golf. No pool. Chamcar/Hertz car hire agency. 100 suites with kitchenettes. In summer full of Gulf families.
PO Box 1097. Tel: (041) 428 700. Email: chamresa@net.sy. www.chamhotels.com

Meridien ★★★
Huge place on its own

spit, 215 rooms, 28 suites and 26 chalets. Like its own world, with a parade of shops, bank, internet café, business centre and hairdresser. Pool, water sports, tennis courts, four restaurants and a bar as well.
PO Box 473. Tel: (041) 428 736. Email: merlatco@net.sy. www.lattakia.lemeridien.com

Sofitel Afamia Tourist Resort ★★★
Closer into Lattakia city centre, just 2km (1¼ miles) to the north, a huge complex with 246 rooms and 42 chalet apartments. Huge pool, marina, jetty and water sports.
Tel: (041) 317 405. www.sofitel.com

Eating out

City Café ★
In a side street just north of the museum grounds just off the corniche, this is a fashionable place with no alcohol but good international fare like pasta and pizzas.
Open: 10am–late.

Plaza Restaurant ★★
North of the museum by 100m (110yds), the Plaza is on the corniche, with a balcony. Serves alcohol and upmarket Arabic and international cuisine.
Open: from 8pm.

Entertainment

The hotels on the Côte d'Azur north of Lattakia offer nightclubs and live music in season. Evening strolling en masse is the family entertainment.

Sport and leisure

Water sports are on offer at the Côte d'Azur beach hotels. The Sofitel Afamia offers windsurfing, pedaloes, water scooters and kayaks.

Mashta Al-Helu

Accommodation

Mashta Al-Helu Resort Hotel ★★★
A good base for mountain walking, this incongruous place looks like a giant Swiss chalet, with a definite Alpine flavour. Its 185 rooms get very full in summer high season with visiting Gulf families and Syrians fleeing the heat of the cities.
Tel: (043) 584 000.

Safita

Accommodation

Safita Cham Hotel ★★★
Like Bosra's version, this is a small and simple member of the Cham Palace Hotel group, with just 50 rooms. In the centre of town, it has little to recommend it except its pool and terrace, but has no competition in the area.
PO Box 25. Tel: (043) 531 131. www.chamhotels.com

Tartous

Accommodation

Shahin Tower Hotel ★★
Busy hotel on the corniche, usually full of businessmen. 156 rooms with balconies and views of Arwad Island.
Tel: (043) 329 100. www.shahinhotels.com

Eating out

Sea Whispers Restaurant ★★
The best of the cluster of fish restaurants along the seafront. Fish remains more expensive than meat because of rarity and only the small boats are allowed to catch fish. Alcohol is served.

Index